WRITINGS OF
THE APOSTOLIC FATHERS:
MATHETES, POLYCARP,
BARNABAS, AND PAPIAS

WRITINGS OF
THE APOSTOLIC FATHERS:
MATHETES, POLYCARP,
BARNABAS, AND PAPIAS

Edited by
Alexander Roberts, D.D.
&
James Donaldson, LL.D.

Revised and Chronologically Arranged, With Brief
Prefaces and Occasional Notes by
A. Cleveland Coxe, D.D.

Edited and re-typeset by
Paul A. Böer, Sr.

VERITATIS SPLENDOR PUBLICATIONS
et cognoscetis veritatem et veritas liberabit vos (Jn 8:32)

MMXIV

The text of this book is excerpted from:

Ante-Nicene Fathers, Vol. 1. Edited by Alexander Roberts, James Donaldson, and A. Cleveland Coxe. Translated by Alexander Roberts and James Donaldson. (Buffalo, NY: Christian Literature Publishing Co., 1885.)

The text of this work is in the public domain.

Retypeset and republished in 2014 by Veritatis Splendor Publications.

CONTENTS

ANTE-NICENE FATHERS

Volume 1

The Apostolic Fathers, Justin Martyr, Irenaeus

Edited by

Alexander Roberts, D.D.

&

James Donaldson, LL.D.

revised and chronologically arranged, with brief

prefaces and occasional notes by

A Cleveland Coxe, D.D.

Mathetes

Introductory Note to the Epistle of Mathetes to Diognetus

[a.d. 130.] The anonymous author of this Epistle gives himself the title (Mathetes) "a disciple [263] of the Apostles," and I venture to adopt it as his name. It is about all we know of him, and it serves a useful end. I place his letter here, as a sequel to the Clementine Epistle, for several reasons, which I think scholars will approve: (1) It is full of the Pauline spirit, and exhales the same pure and primitive fragrance which is characteristic of Clement. (2) No theory as to its date very much conflicts with that which I adopt, and it is sustained by good authorities. (3) But, as a specimen of the persuasives against Gentilism which early Christians employed in their intercourse with friends who adhered to heathenism, it admirably illustrates the temper prescribed by St. Paul (2 Tim. ii. 24), and not less the peculiar social relations of converts to the Gospel with the more amiable and candid of their personal friends at this early period.

Mathetes was possibly a catechumen of St. Paul or of one of the apostle's associates. I assume that his correspondent was the tutor of M. Aurelius. Placed just here, it fills a lacuna in the series, and takes the place of the pseudo (second) Epistle of Clement, which is now relegated to its proper place with the works falsely ascribed to St. Clement.

Altogether, the Epistle is a gem of purest ray; and, while suggesting some difficulties as to interpretation and exposition, it is practically clear as to argument and intent. Mathetes is, perhaps, the first of the apologists.

The following is the original Introductory Notice of the learned editors and translators:--

The following interesting and eloquent Epistle is anonymous, and we have no clue whatever as to its author. For a considerable period after its publication in 1592, it was generally ascribed to Justin Martyr. In recent times Otto has inserted it among the works of that writer, but Semisch and others contend that it cannot possibly be his. In dealing with this question, we depend entirely upon the internal evidence, no statement as to the authorship of the Epistle having descended to us from antiquity. And it can scarcely be denied that the whole tone of the Epistle, as well as special passages which it contains, points to some other writer than Justin. Accordingly, critics are now for the most part agreed that it is not his, and that it must be ascribed to one who lived at a still earlier date in the history of the Church. Several internal arguments have been brought forward in favour of this opinion. Supposing chap. xi. to be genuine, it has been supported by the fact that the writer there styles himself "a disciple of the apostles." But there is great suspicion that the two concluding chapters are spurious; and even though admitted to be genuine, the expression quoted evidently admits of a different explanation from that which implies the writer's personal acquaintance with the apostles: it might, indeed, be adopted by one even at the present day. More weight is to be attached to those passages in which the writer speaks of Christianity as still being a new thing in the world. Expressions to this effect occur in several places (chap. i., ii., ix.), and seem to imply that the author lived very little, if at all, after the apostolic age. There is certainly nothing in the Epistle which is inconsistent with this opinion; and we may therefore believe, that in this beautiful composition we possess a genuine production of some apostolic man who lived not later than the beginning of the second century.

The names of Clement of Rome and of Apollos have both been suggested as those of the probable author. Such opinions, however, are pure fancies, which it is perhaps impossible to refute, but which rest on nothing more than conjecture. Nor can a single word be said as to the person named Diognetus, to whom the letter is addressed. We must be content to leave both points in hopeless obscurity, and simply accept the Epistle as written by an earnest and intelligent Christian to a sincere inquirer among the Gentiles, towards the close of the apostolic age.

It is much to be regretted that the text is often so very doubtful. Only three mss. of the Epistle, all probably exhibiting the same original text, are known to exist; and in not a few passages the readings are, in consequence, very defective and obscure. But notwithstanding this drawback, and the difficulty of representing the full force and elegance of the original, this Epistle, as now presented to the English reader, can hardly fail to excite both his deepest interest and admiration.

[N.B.--Interesting speculations concerning this precious work may be seen in Bunsen's Hippolytus and his Age, vol. i. p. 188. The learned do not seem convinced by this author, but I have adopted his suggestion as to Diognetus the tutor of M. Aurelius.]

[263] apostolon genomenos mathetes. Cap. xi.

The Epistle of Mathetes to Diognetus

Chapter I.--Occasion of the epistle.

Since I see thee, most excellent Diognetus, exceedingly desirous to learn the mode of worshipping God prevalent among the Christians, and inquiring very carefully and earnestly concerning them, what God they trust in, and what form of religion they observe, [264] so as all to look down upon the world itself, and despise death, while they neither esteem those to be gods that are reckoned such by the Greeks, nor hold to the superstition of the Jews; and what is the affection which they cherish among themselves; and why, in fine, this new kind or practice [of piety] has only now entered into the world, [265] and not long ago; I cordially welcome this thy desire, and I implore God, who enables us both to speak and to hear, to grant to me so to speak, that, above all, I may hear you have been edified, [266] and to you so to hear, that I who speak may have no cause of regret for having done so.

[264] Literally, "trusting in what God, etc., they look down."

[265] Or, "life."

[266] Some read, "that you by hearing may be edified."

Chapter II.--The vanity of idols.

Come, then, after you have freed [267] yourself from all prejudices possessing your mind, and laid aside what you have been accustomed to, as something apt to deceive [268] you, and being made, as if from the beginning, a new man,

18

inasmuch as, according to your own confession, you are to
be the hearer of a new [system of] doctrine; come and
contemplate, not with your eyes only, but with your
understanding, the substance and the form [269] of those
whom ye declare and deem to be gods. Is not one of them a
stone similar to that on which we tread? Is [270] not a
second brass, in no way superior to those vessels which are
constructed for our ordinary use? Is not a third wood, and
that already rotten? Is not a fourth silver, which needs a
man to watch it, lest it be stolen? Is not a fifth iron,
consumed by rust? Is not a sixth earthenware, in no degree
more valuable than that which is formed for the humblest
purposes? Are not all these of corruptible matter? Are they
not fabricated by means of iron and fire? Did not the
sculptor fashion one of them, the brazier a second, the
silversmith a third, and the potter a fourth? Was not every
one of them, before they were formed by the arts of these
[workmen] into the shape of these [gods], each in its [271]
own way subject to change? Would not those things which
are now vessels, formed of the same materials, become like
to such, if they met with the same artificers? Might not
these, which are now worshipped by you, again be made by
men vessels similar to others? Are they not all deaf? Are
they not blind? Are they not without life? Are they not
destitute of feeling? Are they not incapable of motion? Are
they not all liable to rot? Are they not all corruptible? These
things ye call gods; these ye serve; these ye worship; and ye
become altogether like to them. For this reason ye hate the
Christians, because they do not deem these to be gods. But
do not ye yourselves, who now think and suppose [such to
be gods], much more cast contempt upon them than they
[the Christians do]? Do ye not much more mock and insult

them, when ye worship those that are made of stone and earthenware, without appointing any persons to guard them; but those made of silver and gold ye shut up by night, and appoint watchers to look after them by day, lest they be stolen? And by those gifts which ye mean to present to them, do ye not, if they are possessed of sense, rather punish [than honour] them? But if, on the other hand, they are destitute of sense, ye convict them of this fact, while ye worship them with blood and the smoke of sacrifices. Let any one of you suffer such indignities! [272] Let any one of you endure to have such things done to himself! But not a single human being will, unless compelled to it, endure such treatment, since he is endowed with sense and reason. A stone, however, readily bears it, seeing it is insensible. Certainly you do not show [by your [273] conduct] that he [your God] is possessed of sense. And as to the fact that Christians are not accustomed to serve such gods, I might easily find many other things to say; but if even what has been said does not seem to any one sufficient, I deem it idle to say anything further.

[267] Or, "purified."

[268] Literally, "which is deceiving."

[269] Literally, "of what substance, or of what form."

[270] Some make this and the following clauses affirmative instead of interrogative.

[271] The text is here corrupt. Several attempts at emendation have been made, but without any marked success.

[272] Some read, "Who of you would tolerate these things?" etc.

[273] The text is here uncertain, and the sense obscure. The meaning seems to be, that by sprinkling their gods with blood, etc., they tended to prove that these were not possessed of sense.

Chapter III.--Superstitions of the Jews.

And next, I imagine that you are most desirous of hearing something on this point, that the Christians do not observe the same forms of divine worship as do the Jews. The Jews, then, if they abstain from the kind of service above described, and deem it proper to worship one God as being Lord of all, [are right]; but if they offer Him worship in the way which we have described, they greatly err. For while the Gentiles, by offering such things to those that are destitute of sense and hearing, furnish an example of madness; they, on the other hand, by thinking to offer these things to God as if He needed them, might justly reckon it rather an act of folly than of divine worship. For He that made heaven and earth, and all that is therein, and gives to us all the things of which we stand in need, certainly requires none of those things which He Himself bestows on such as think of furnishing them to Him. But those who imagine that, by means of blood, and the smoke of sacrifices and burnt-offerings, they offer sacrifices [acceptable] to Him, and that by such honours they show Him respect, --these, by [274] supposing that they can give anything to Him who stands in need of nothing, appear to me in no respect to differ from those who studiously confer the same honour on things destitute of sense, and which therefore are unable to enjoy such honours.

[274] The text here is very doubtful. We have followed that adopted by most critics.

Chapter IV.--The other observances of the Jews.

But as to their scrupulosity concerning meats, and their superstition as respects the Sabbaths, and their boasting about circumcision, and their fancies about fasting and the new moons, which are utterly ridiculous and unworthy of notice,--I do not [275] think that you require to learn anything from me. For, to accept some of those things which have been formed by God for the use of men as properly formed, and to reject others as useless and redundant,--how can this be lawful? And to speak falsely of God, as if He forbade us to do what is good on the Sabbath-days,--how is not this impious? And to glory in the circumcision [276] of the flesh as a proof of election, and as if, on account of it, they were specially beloved by God,-- how is it not a subject of ridicule? And as to their observing months and days, [277] as if waiting upon [278] the stars and the moon, and their distributing, [279] according to their own tendencies, the appointments of God, and the vicissitudes of the seasons, some for festivities, [280] and others for mourning,--who would deem this a part of divine worship, and not much rather a manifestation of folly? I suppose, then, you are sufficiently convinced that the Christians properly abstain from the vanity and error common [to both Jews and Gentiles], and from the busy-body spirit and vain boasting of the Jews; but you must not hope to learn the mystery of their peculiar mode of worshipping God from any mortal.

[275] Otto, resting on ms. authority, omits the negative, but the sense seems to require its insertion.

[276] Literally, "lessening."

[277] Comp. Gal. iv. 10.

[278] This seems to refer to the practice of Jews in fixing the beginning of the day, and consequently of the Sabbath, from the rising of the stars. They used to say, that when three stars of moderate magnitude appeared, it was night; when two, it was twilight; and when only one, that day had not yet departed. It thus came to pass (according to their night-day (nuchthemeron) reckoning), that whosoever engaged in work on the evening of Friday, the beginning of the Sabbath, after three stars of moderate size were visible, was held to have sinned, and had to present a trespass-offering; and so on, according to the fanciful rule described.

[279] Otto supplies the lacuna which here occurs in the mss. so as to read katadiairein.

[280] The great festivals of the Jews are here referred to on the one hand, and the day of atonement on the other.

Chapter V.--The manners of the Christians.

For the Christians are distinguished from other men neither by country, nor language, nor the customs which they observe. For they neither inhabit cities of their own, nor employ a peculiar form of speech, nor lead a life which is

marked out by any singularity. The course of conduct which
they follow has not been devised by any speculation or
deliberation of inquisitive men; nor do they, like some,
proclaim themselves the advocates of any merely human
doctrines. But, inhabiting Greek as well as barbarian cities,
according as the lot of each of them has determined, and
following the customs of the natives in respect to clothing,
food, and the rest of their ordinary conduct, they display to
us their wonderful and confessedly striking [281] method of
life. They dwell in their own countries, but simply as
sojourners. As citizens, they share in all things with others,
and yet endure all things as if foreigners. Every foreign land
is to them as their native country, and every land of their
birth as a land of strangers. They marry, as do all [others];
they beget children; but they do not destroy their offspring.
[282] They have a common table, but not a common bed.
[283] They are in the flesh, but they do not live after the
flesh. [284] They pass their days on earth, but they are
citizens of heaven. [285] They obey the prescribed laws, and
at the same time surpass the laws by their lives. They love
all men, and are persecuted by all. They are unknown and
condemned; they are put to death, and restored to life. [286]
They are poor, yet make many rich; [287] they are in lack of
all things, and yet abound in all; they are dishonoured, and
yet in their very dishonour are glorified. They are evil
spoken of, and yet are justified; they are reviled, and bless;
[288] they are insulted, and repay the insult with honour;
they do good, yet are punished as evil-doers. When
punished, they rejoice as if quickened into life; they are
assailed by the Jews as foreigners, and are persecuted by the
Greeks; yet those who hate them are unable to assign any
reason for their hatred.

[281] Literally, "paradoxical."

[282] Literally, "cast away foetuses."

[283] Otto omits "bed," which is an emendation, and gives the second "common" the sense of unclean.

[284] Comp. 2 Cor. x. 3.

[285] Comp. Phil. iii. 20.

[286] Comp. 2 Cor. vi. 9.

[287] Comp. 2 Cor. vi. 10.

[288] Comp. 2 Cor. iv. 12.

Chapter VI.--The relation of Christians to the world.

To sum up all in one word--what the soul is in the body, that are Christians in the world. The soul is dispersed through all the members of the body, and Christians are scattered through all the cities of the world. The soul dwells in the body, yet is not of the body; and Christians dwell in the world, yet are not of the world. [289] The invisible soul is guarded by the visible body, and Christians are known indeed to be in the world, but their godliness remains invisible. The flesh hates the soul, and wars against it, [290] though itself suffering no injury, because it is prevented from enjoying pleasures; the world also hates the Christians, though in nowise injured, because they abjure pleasures. The soul loves the flesh that hates it, and [loves also] the members; Christians likewise love those that hate them. The soul is imprisoned in the body, yet preserves [291] that very body; and Christians are confined in the world as in a prison, and yet they are the preservers [292] of the world. The immortal soul dwells in a mortal tabernacle; and Christians dwell as sojourners in corruptible [bodies], looking for an incorruptible dwelling [293] in the heavens. The soul, when but ill-provided with food and drink, becomes better; in like manner, the Christians, though subjected day by day to punishment, increase the more in number. [294] God has assigned them this illustrious position, which it were unlawful for them to forsake.

[289] John xvii. 11, 14, 16.

[290] Comp. 1 Pet. ii. 11.

[291] Literally, "keeps together."

[292] Literally, "keeps together."

[293] Literally, "incorruption."

[294] Or, "though punished, increase in number daily."

Chapter VII.--The manifestation of Christ.

For, as I said, this was no mere earthly invention which was delivered to them, nor is it a mere human system of opinion, which they judge it right to preserve so carefully, nor has a dispensation of mere human mysteries been committed to them, but truly God Himself, who is almighty, the Creator of all things, and invisible, has sent from heaven, and placed among men, [Him who is] the truth, and the holy and incomprehensible Word, and has firmly established Him in their hearts. He did not, as one might have imagined, send to men any servant, or angel, or ruler, or any one of those who bear sway over earthly things, or one of those to whom the government of things in the heavens has been entrusted, but the very Creator and Fashioner of all things--by whom He made the heavens--by whom he enclosed the sea within its proper bounds--whose ordinances [295] all the stars [296] faithfully observe--from whom the sun [297] has received the measure of his daily course to be observed [298] -- whom the moon obeys, being commanded to shine in the night, and whom the stars also obey, following the moon in her course; by whom all things have been arranged, and placed within their proper limits, and to whom all are subject--the heavens and the things that are therein, the earth and the things that are therein, the sea and the things that are therein--fire, air, and the abyss--the things which are in the heights, the things which are in the depths, and the things which lie between. This [messenger] He sent to them. Was it then, as one [299] might conceive, for the purpose of exercising tyranny, or of inspiring fear and terror? By no means, but under the influence of clemency and meekness. As a king sends his son, who is also a king, so sent He Him; as God [300] He sent Him; as to men He sent Him; as a Saviour He sent Him, and as seeking to persuade, not to compel us; for violence has no place in the character of God. As calling us He sent Him, not as vengefully pursuing us; as loving us He sent Him, not as judging us. For He will yet send Him to judge us, and who shall endure His appearing? [301] ... Do you not see them exposed to wild beasts, that they may be persuaded to deny the Lord, and yet not overcome? Do you not see that the more of them are punished, the greater becomes the number of the rest? This does not seem to be the work of man: this is the power of God; these are the evidences of His manifestation.

[295] Literally, "mysteries."

[296] Literally, "elements."

[297] The word "sun," though omitted in the mss., should manifestly be inserted.

[298] Literally, "has received to observe."

[299] Literally, "one of men."

[300] "God" here refers to the person sent.

[301] [Comp. Mal. iii. 2. The Old Testament is frequently in mind, if not expressly quoted by Mathetes.] A considerable gap here occurs in the mss.

Chapter VIII.--The miserable state of men before the coming of the Word.

For, who of men at all understood before His coming what God is? Do you accept of the vain and silly doctrines of those who are deemed trustworthy philosophers? of whom some said that fire was God, calling that God to which they themselves were by and by to come; and some water; and others some other of the elements formed by God. But if any one of these theories be worthy of approbation, every one of the rest of created things might also be declared to be God. But such declarations are simply the startling and erroneous utterances of deceivers; [302] and no man has either seen Him, or made Him known, [303] but He has revealed Himself. And He has manifested Himself through faith, to which alone it is given to behold God. For God, the Lord and Fashioner of all things, who made all things, and assigned them their several positions, proved Himself not merely a friend of mankind, but also long-suffering [in His dealings with them]. Yea, He was always of such a character, and still is, and will ever be, kind and good, and free from wrath, and true, and the only one who is [absolutely] good; [304] and He formed in His mind a great and unspeakable conception, which He communicated to His Son alone. As long, then, as He held and preserved His own wise counsel in concealment, [305] He appeared to neglect us, and to have no care over us. But after He revealed and laid open, through His beloved Son, the things which had been prepared from the beginning, He conferred every blessing [306] all at once upon us, so that we should both share in His benefits, and see and be active [307] [in His service]. Who of us would ever have expected these things? He was aware, then, of all things in His own mind, along with His Son, according to the relation [308] subsisting between them.

[302] Literally, "these things are the marvels and error."

[303] Or, "known Him."

[304] Comp. Matt. xix. 17.

[305] Literally, "in a mystery."

[306] Literally, "all things."

[307] The sense is here very obscure. We have followed the text of Otto, who fills up the lacuna in the ms. as above. Others have, "to see, and to handle Him."

[308] Literally, "economically."

Chapter IX.--Why the Son was sent so late.

As long then as the former time [309] endured, He permitted us to be borne along by unruly impulses, being drawn away by the desire of pleasure and various lusts. This was not that He at all delighted in our sins, but that He simply endured them; nor that He approved the time of working iniquity which then was, but that He sought to form a mind conscious of righteousness, [310] so that being convinced in that time of our unworthiness of attaining life through our own works, it should now, through the kindness of God, be vouchsafed to us; and having made it manifest that in ourselves we were unable to enter into the kingdom of God, we might through the power of God be made able. But when our wickedness had reached its height, and it had been clearly shown that its reward, [311] punishment and death, was impending over us; and when the time had come which God had before appointed for manifesting His own kindness and power, how [312] the one love of God, through exceeding regard for men, did not regard us with hatred, nor thrust us away, nor remember our iniquity against us, but showed great long-suffering, and bore with us, [313] He Himself took on Him the burden of our iniquities, He gave His own Son as a ransom for us, the holy One for transgressors, the blameless One for the wicked, the righteous One for the unrighteous, the incorruptible One for the corruptible, the immortal One for them that are mortal. For what other thing was capable of covering our sins than His righteousness? By what other one was it possible that we, the wicked and ungodly, could be justified, than by the only Son of God? O sweet exchange! O unsearchable operation! O benefits surpassing all expectation! that the wickedness of many should be hid in a single righteous One, and that the righteousness of One should justify many transgressors! [314] Having therefore convinced us in the former time [315] that our nature was unable to attain to life, and having now revealed the Saviour who is able to save even those things which it was [formerly] impossible to save, by both these facts He desired to lead us to trust in His kindness, to esteem Him our Nourisher, Father, Teacher, Counsellor, Healer, our Wisdom, Light, Honour, Glory, Power, and Life, so that we should not be anxious [316] concerning clothing and food.

[309] Otto refers for a like contrast between these two times to Rom. iii. 21-26, Rom. v. 20 and Gal. iv. 4. [Comp. Acts xvii. 30.]

[310] The reading and sense are doubtful.

[311] Both the text and rendering are here somewhat doubtful, but the sense will in any case be much the same.

[312] Many variations here occur in the way in which the lacuna of the mss. is to be supplied. They do not, however, greatly affect the meaning.

[313] In the ms. "saying" is here inserted, as if the words had been regarded as a quotation from Isa. liii. 11.

[314] [See Bossuet, who quotes it as from Justin Martyr (Tom. iii. p. 171). Sermon on Circumcision.]

[315] That is, before Christ appeared.

[316] Comp. Matt. vi. 25, etc. [Mathetes, in a single sentence, expounds a most practical text with comprehensive views.]

Chapter X.--The blessings that will flow from faith.

If you also desire [to possess] this faith, you likewise shall receive first of all the knowledge of the Father. [317] For God has loved mankind, on whose account He made the world, to whom He rendered subject all the things that are in it, [318] to whom He gave reason and understanding, to whom alone He imparted the privilege of looking upwards to Himself, whom He formed after His own image, to whom He sent His only-begotten Son, to whom He has promised a kingdom in heaven, and will give it to those who have loved Him. And when you have attained this knowledge, with what joy do you think you will be filled? Or, how will you love Him who has first so loved you? And if you love Him, you will be an imitator of His kindness. And do not wonder that a man may become an imitator of God. He can, if he is willing. For it is not by ruling over his neighbours, or by seeking to hold the supremacy over those that are weaker, or by being rich, and showing violence towards those that are inferior, that happiness is found; nor can any one by these things become an imitator of God. But these things do not at all constitute His majesty. On the contrary he who takes upon himself the burden of his neighbour; he who, in whatsoever respect he may be superior, is ready to benefit another who is deficient; he who, whatsoever things he has received from God, by distributing these to the needy, becomes a god to those who receive [his benefits]: he is an imitator of God. Then thou shalt see, while still on earth, that God in the heavens rules over [the universe]; then thou shall begin to speak the mysteries of God; then shalt thou both love and admire those that suffer punishment because they will not deny God; then shall thou condemn the deceit and error of the world when thou shall know what it is to live truly in heaven, when thou shalt despise that which is here esteemed to be death, when thou shalt fear what is truly death, which is reserved for those who shall be condemned to the eternal fire, which shall afflict those even to the end that are committed to it. Then shalt thou admire those who for righteousness' sake endure the fire that is but for a moment, and shalt count them happy when thou shalt know [the nature of] that fire.

 [317] Thus Otto supplies the lacuna; others conjecture somewhat different supplements.

[318] So Böhl. Sylburgius and Otto read, "in the earth."

Chapter XI.--These things are worthy to be known and believed.

I do not speak of things strange to me, nor do I aim at anything inconsistent with right reason; [319] but having been a disciple of the Apostles, I am become a teacher of the Gentiles. I minister the things delivered to me to those that are disciples worthy of the truth. For who that is rightly taught and begotten by the loving [320] Word, would not seek to learn accurately the things which have been clearly shown by the Word to His disciples, to whom the Word being manifested has revealed them, speaking plainly [to them], not understood indeed by the unbelieving, but conversing with the disciples, who, being esteemed faithful by Him, acquired a knowledge of the mysteries of the Father? For which [321] reason He sent the Word, that He might be manifested to the world; and He, being despised by the people [of the Jews], was, when preached by the Apostles, believed on by the Gentiles. [322] This is He who was from the beginning, who appeared as if new, and was found old, and yet who is ever born afresh in the hearts of the saints. This is He who, being from everlasting, is to-day called [323] the Son; through whom the Church is enriched, and grace, widely spread, increases in the saints, furnishing understanding, revealing mysteries, announcing times, rejoicing over the faithful, giving [324] to those that seek, by whom the limits of faith are not broken through, nor the boundaries set by the fathers passed over. Then the fear of the law is chanted, and the grace of the prophets is known, and the faith of the gospels is established, and the tradition of the Apostles is preserved, and the grace of the Church exults; which grace if you grieve not, you shall know those things which the Word teaches, by whom He wills, and when He pleases. For whatever things we are moved to utter by the will of the Word commanding us, we communicate to you with pains, and from a love of the things that have been revealed to us.

[319] Some render, "nor do I rashly seek to persuade others."

[320] Some propose to read, "and becoming a friend to the Word."

[321] It has been proposed to connect this with the preceding sentence, and read, "have known the mysteries of the Father, viz., for what purpose He sent the Word."

[322] [Comp. 1 Tim. iii. 16.]

[323] Or, "esteemed."

[324] Or, "given."

Chapter XII.--The importance of knowledge to true spiritual life.

When you have read and carefully listened to these things, you shall know what God bestows on such as rightly love Him, being made [as ye are] a paradise of delight, presenting [325] in yourselves a tree bearing all kinds of produce and flourishing well, being adorned with various fruits. For in this place [326] the tree of knowledge and the tree of life have been planted; but it is not the tree of knowledge that destroys-- it is disobedience that proves destructive. Nor truly are those words without significance which are written, how God from the beginning planted the tree of life in the midst of paradise, revealing through knowledge the way to life, [327] and when those who were first formed did not use this [knowledge] properly, they were, through the fraud of the Serpent, stripped naked. [328] For neither can life exist without knowledge, nor is knowledge secure without life. Wherefore both were planted close together. The Apostle, perceiving the force [of this conjunction], and blaming that knowledge which, without true doctrine, is admitted to influence life, [329] declares, "Knowledge puffeth up, but love edifieth." For he who thinks he knows anything without true knowledge, and such as is witnessed to by life, knows nothing, but is deceived by the Serpent, as not [330] loving life. But he who combines knowledge with fear, and seeks after life, plants in hope, looking for fruit. Let your heart be your wisdom; and let your life be true knowledge [331] inwardly received. Bearing this tree and displaying its fruit, thou shalt always gather [332] in those things which are desired by God, which the Serpent cannot reach, and to which deception does not approach; nor is Eve then corrupted, [333] but is trusted as a virgin; and salvation is manifested, and the Apostles are filled with understanding, and the Passover [334] of the Lord advances, and the choirs [335] are gathered together, and are arranged in proper order, and the Word rejoices in teaching the saints,--by whom the Father is glorified: to whom be glory for ever. Amen. [336]

[325] Literally, "bringing forth."

[326] That is, in Paradise.

[327] Literally "revealing life."

[328] Or, "deprived of it."

[329] Literally, "knowledge without the truth of a command exercised to life." See 1 Cor. viii. 1.

[330] The ms. is here defective. Some read, "on account of the love of life."

[331] Or, "true word," or "reason."

[332] Or, "reap."

[333] The meaning seems to be, that if the tree of true knowledge and life be planted within you, you shall continue free from blemishes and sins.

[334] [This looks like a reference to the Apocalypse, Rev. v. 9., Rev. xix. 7., Rev. xx. 5.]

[335] Here Bishop Wordsworth would read kleroi, cites 1 Pet. v. 3, and refers to Suicer (Lexicon) in voce kleros.]

[336] [Note the Clement-like doxology.]

Polycarp

Introductory Note to the Epistle of Polycarp to the Philippians

[a.d. 65-100-155.] The Epistle of Polycarp is usually made a sort of preface to those of Ignatius, for reasons which will be obvious to the reader. Yet he was born later, and lived to a much later period. They seem to have been friends from the days of their common pupilage under St. John; and there is nothing improbable in the conjecture of Usher, that he was the "angel of the church in Smyrna," to whom the Master says, "Be thou faithful unto death, and I will give thee a crown of life." His pupil Irenæus gives us one of the very few portraits of an apostolic man which are to be found in antiquity, in a few sentences which are a picture: "I could describe the very place in which the blessed Polycarp sat and taught; his going out and coming in; the whole tenor of his life; his personal appearance; how he would speak of the conversations he had held with John and with others who had seen the Lord. How did he make mention of their words and of whatever he had heard from them respecting the Lord." Thus he unconsciously tantalizes our reverent curiosity. Alas! that such conversations were not written for our learning. But there is a wise Providence in what is withheld, as well as in the inestimable treasures we have received.

Irenæus will tell us more concerning him, his visit to Rome, his rebuke of Marcion, and incidental anecdotes, all which are instructive. The expression which he applied to Marcion is found in this Epistle. Other facts of interest are found in the Martyrdom, which follows in these pages. His death, in extreme old age under the first of the Antonines, has been variously dated; but we may accept the date we have given, as rendered probable by that of the Paschal question, which he so lovingly settled with Anicetus, Bishop of Rome.

The Epistle to the Philippians is the more interesting as denoting the state of that beloved church, the firstborn of European churches, and so greatly endeared to St. Paul. It abounds in practical wisdom, and is rich in Scripture and Scriptural allusions. It reflects the spirit of St. John, alike in its lamb-like and its aquiline features: he is as loving as the beloved disciple himself when he speaks of Christ and his church, but "the son of thunder" is echoed in his rebukes of threatened corruptions in faith and morals. Nothing can be more clear than his view of the doctrines of grace; but he writes like the disciple of St. John, though in perfect harmony with St. Paul's hymn-like eulogy of Christian love.

The following is the original Introductory Notice:--

The authenticity of the following Epistle can on no fair grounds be questioned. It is abundantly established by external testimony, and is also supported by the internal evidence. Irenæus says (Adv. Hær., iii. 3): "There is extant an Epistle of Polycarp written to the Philippians, most satisfactory, from which those that have a mind to do so may learn the character of his faith," etc. This passage is embodied by Eusebius in his Ecclesiastical History (iv. 14); and in another place the same writer refers to the Epistle before us as an undoubted production of Polycarp (Hist. Eccl., iii. 36). Other ancient testimonies might easily be added, but are superfluous, inasmuch as there is a general consent among scholars at the present day that we have in this letter an authentic production of the renowned Bishop of Smyrna.

Of Polycarp's life little is known, but that little is highly interesting. Irenæus was his disciple, and tells us that "Polycarp was instructed by the apostles, and was brought into contact with many who had seen Christ" (Adv. Hær., iii. 3; Euseb. Hist. Eccl., iv. 14). There is also a very graphic account given of Polycarp by Irenæus in his Epistle to Florinus, to which the reader is referred. It has been preserved by Eusebius (Hist. Eccl., v. 20).

The Epistle before us is not perfect in any of the Greek mss. which contain it. But the chapters wanting in Greek are contained in an ancient Latin version. While there is no ground for supposing, as some have done, that the whole Epistle is spurious, there seems considerable force in the arguments by which many others have sought to prove chap. xiii. to be an interpolation.

The date of the Epistle cannot be satisfactorily determined. It depends on the conclusion we reach as to some points, very difficult and obscure, connected with that account of the martyrdom of Polycarp which has come down to us. We shall not, however, probably be far wrong if we fix it about the middle of the second century.

The Epistle of Polycarp to the Philippians [337]

Polycarp, and the presbyters [338] with him, to the Church of God sojourning at Philippi: Mercy to you, and peace from God Almighty, and from the Lord Jesus Christ, our Saviour, be multiplied.

Chapter I.--Praise of the Philippians.

I have greatly rejoiced with you in our Lord Jesus Christ, because ye have followed the example [339] of true love [as displayed by God], and have accompanied, as became you, those who were bound in chains, the fitting ornaments of saints, and which are indeed the diadems of the true elect of God and our Lord; and because the strong root of your faith, spoken of in days [340] long gone by, endureth even until now, and bringeth forth fruit to our Lord Jesus Christ, who for our sins suffered even unto death, [but] "whom God raised from the dead, having loosed the bands of the grave." [341] "In whom, though now ye see Him not, ye believe, and believing, rejoice with joy unspeakable and full of glory;" [342] into which joy many desire to enter, knowing that "by grace ye are saved, not of works," [343] but by the will of God through Jesus Christ.

[339] Literally, "ye have received the patterns of true love."

[340] Phil. i. 5.

[341] Acts ii. 24. Literally, "having loosed the pains of Hades."

[342] 1 Pet. i. 8.

[343] Eph. ii. 8, 9.

Chapter II.--An exhortation to virtue.

"Wherefore, girding up your loins," [344] "serve the Lord in fear" [345] and truth, as those who have forsaken the vain, empty talk and error of the multitude, and "believed in Him who raised up our Lord Jesus Christ from the dead, and gave Him glory," [346] and a throne at His right hand. To Him all things [347] in heaven and on earth are subject. Him every spirit serves. He comes as the Judge of the living and the dead. [348] His blood will God require of those who do not believe in Him. [349] But He who raised Him up from the dead will raise [350] up us also, if we do His will, and walk in His commandments, and love what He loved, keeping ourselves from all unrighteousness, covetousness, love of money, evil speaking, false witness; "not rendering evil for evil, or railing for railing," [351] or blow for blow, or cursing for cursing, but being mindful of what the Lord said in His teaching: "Judge not, that ye be not judged; [352] forgive, and it shall be forgiven unto you; [353] be merciful, that ye may obtain mercy; [354] with what measure ye mete, it shall be measured to you again;" [355] and once more, "Blessed are the poor, and those that are persecuted for righteousness' sake, for theirs is the kingdom of God." [356]

[344] Comp. 1 Pet. i. 13; Eph. vi. 14.

[345] Ps. ii. 11.

[346] 1 Pet. i. 21.

[347] Comp. 1 Pet. iii. 22; Phil. ii. 10.

[348] Comp. Acts xvii. 31.

[349] Or, "who do not obey him."

[350] Comp 1 Cor. vi. 14; 2 Cor. iv. 14; Rom. viii. 11.

[351] 1 Pet. iii. 9.

[352] Matt. vii. 1.

[353] Matt. vi. 12, 14; Luke vi. 37.

[354] Luke vi. 36.

[355] Matt. vii. 2; Luke vi. 38.

[356] Matt. v. 3, 10; Luke vi. 20.

Chapter III.--Expressions of personal unworthiness.

These things, brethren, I write to you concerning righteousness, not because I take anything upon myself, but because ye have invited me to do so. For neither I, nor any other such one, can come up to the wisdom [357] of the blessed and glorified Paul. He, when among you, accurately and stedfastly taught the word of truth in the presence of those who were then alive. And when absent from you, he wrote you a letter, [358] which, if you carefully study, you will find to be the means of building you up in that faith which has been given you, and which, being followed by hope, and preceded by love towards God, and Christ, and our neighbour, "is the mother of us all." [359] For if any one be inwardly possessed of these graces, he hath fulfilled the command of righteousness, since he that hath love is far from all sin.

[357] Comp. 2 Pet. iii. 15.

[358] The form is plural, but one Epistle is probably meant. [So, even in English, "letters" may be classically used for a single letter, as we say "by these presents." But even we might speak of St. Paul as having written his Epistles to us;

so the Epistles to Thessalonica and Corinth might more naturally still be referred to here].

[359] Comp. Gal. iv. 26.

Chapter IV.--Various exhortations.

"But the love of money is the root of all evils." [360] Knowing, therefore, that "as we brought nothing into the world, so we can carry nothing out," [361] let us arm ourselves with the armour of righteousness; [362] and let us teach, first of all, ourselves to walk in the commandments of the Lord. Next, [teach] your wives [to walk] in the faith given to them, and in love and purity tenderly loving their own husbands in all truth, and loving all [others] equally in all chastity; and to train up their children in the knowledge and fear of God. Teach the widows to be discreet as respects the faith of the Lord, praying continually [363] for all, being far from all slandering, evil-speaking, false-witnessing, love of money, and every kind of evil; knowing that they are the altar [364] of God, that He clearly perceives all things, and that nothing is hid from Him, neither reasonings, nor reflections, nor any one of the secret things of the heart.

[360] 1 Tim. vi. 10.

[361] 1 Tim. vi. 7.

[362] Comp. Eph. vi. 11.

[363] Comp. 1 Thess. v. 17.

[364] Some here read, "altars."

Chapter V.--The duties of deacons, youths, and virgins.

Knowing, then, that "God is not mocked," [365] we ought to walk worthy of His commandment and glory. In like manner should the deacons be blameless before the face of His righteousness, as being the servants of God and Christ, [366] and not of men. They must not be slanderers, double-tongued, [367] or lovers of money, but temperate in all things, compassionate, industrious, walking according to the truth of the Lord, who was the servant [368] of all. If we please Him in this present world, we shall receive also the future world, according as He has promised to us that He will raise us again from the dead, and that if we live [369] worthily of Him, "we shall also reign together with Him," [370] provided only we believe. In like manner, let the young men also be blameless in all things, being especially careful to preserve purity, and keeping themselves in, as with a bridle, from every kind of evil. For it is well that they should be cut off from [371] the lusts that are in the world, since "every lust warreth against the spirit;" [372] and "neither fornicators, nor effeminate, nor abusers of themselves with mankind, shall inherit the kingdom of God," [373] nor those who do things inconsistent and unbecoming. Wherefore, it is needful to abstain from all these things, being subject to the presbyters and deacons, as unto God and Christ. The virgins also must walk in a blameless and pure conscience.

[365] Gal. vi. 7.

[366] Some read, "God in Christ."

[367] Comp. 1 Tim. iii. 8.

[368] Comp. Matt. xx. 28.

[369] Politeusometha, referring to the whole conduct; comp. Phil. i. 27.

[370] 2 Tim. ii. 12.

[371] Some read, anakuptesthai, "to emerge from." [So Chevallier, but not Wake nor Jacobson. See the note of latter, ad loc.]

[372] 1 Pet. ii. 11.

[373] 1 Cor. vi. 9, 10.

Chapter VI.--The duties of presbyters and others.

And let the presbyters be compassionate and merciful to all, bringing back those that wander, visiting all the sick, and not neglecting the widow, the orphan, or the poor, but always "providing for that which is becoming in the sight of God and man;" [374] abstaining from all wrath, respect of persons, and unjust judgment; keeping far off from all covetousness, not quickly crediting [an evil report] against any one, not severe in judgment, as knowing that we are all under a debt of sin. If then we entreat the Lord to forgive us, we ought also ourselves to forgive; [375] for we are before the eyes of our Lord and God, and "we must all appear at the judgment-seat of Christ, and must every one give an account of himself." [376] Let us then serve Him in fear, and with all reverence, even as He Himself has commanded us, and as the apostles who preached the

Gospel unto us, and the prophets who proclaimed beforehand the coming of the Lord [have alike taught us]. Let us be zealous in the pursuit of that which is good, keeping ourselves from causes of offence, from false brethren, and from those who in hypocrisy bear the name of the Lord, and draw away vain men into error.

[374] Rom. xii. 17; 2 Cor. viii. 31.

[375] Matt. vi. 12-14.

[376] Rom. xiv. 10-12; 2 Cor. v. 10.

Chapter VII.--Avoid the Docetæ, and persevere in fasting and prayer.

"For whosoever does not confess that Jesus Christ has come in the flesh, is antichrist;" [377] and whosoever does not confess the testimony of the cross, [378] is of the devil; and whosoever perverts the oracles of the Lord to his own lusts, and says that there is neither a resurrection nor a judgment, he is the first-born of Satan. [379] Wherefore, forsaking the vanity of many, and their false doctrines, let us return to the word which has been handed down to us from [380] the beginning; "watching unto prayer," [381] and persevering in fasting; beseeching in our supplications the all-seeing God "not to lead us into temptation," [382] as the Lord has said: "The spirit truly is willing, but the flesh is weak." [383]

[377] 1 John iv. 3.

[378] Literally, "the martyrdom of the cross," which some render, "His suffering on the cross."

[379] [The original, perhaps, of Eusebius (Hist. iv. cap. 14). It became a common-place expression in the Church.]

[380] Comp. Jude 3.

[381] 1 Pet. iv. 7.

[382] Matt. vi. 13; Matt. xxvi. 41.

[383] Matt. xxvi. 41; Mark xiv. 38.

Chapter VIII.--Persevere in hope and patience.

Let us then continually persevere in our hope, and the earnest of our righteousness, which is Jesus Christ, "who bore our sins in His own body on the tree," [384] "who did no sin, neither was guile found in His mouth," [385] but endured all things for us, that we might live in Him. [386] Let us then be imitators of His patience; and if we suffer [387] for His name's sake, let us glorify Him. [388] For He has set us this example [389] in Himself, and we have believed that such is the case.

 [384] 1 Pet. ii. 24.

[385] 1 Pet. ii. 22.

[386] Comp. 1 John iv. 9.

[387] Comp. Acts v. 41; 1 Pet. iv. 16.

[388] Some read, "we glorify Him."

[389] Comp. 1 Pet. ii. 21.

Chapter IX.--Patience inculcated.

I exhort you all, therefore, to yield obedience to the word of righteousness, and to exercise all patience, such as ye have seen [set] before your eyes, not only in the case of the blessed Ignatius, and Zosimus, and Rufus, but also in others among yourselves, and in Paul himself, and the rest of the apostles. [This do] in the assurance that all these have not run [390] in vain, but in faith and righteousness, and that they are [now] in their due place in the presence of the Lord, with whom also they suffered. For they loved not this present world, but Him who died for us, and for our sakes was raised again by God from the dead.

[390] Comp. Phil. ii. 16; Gal. ii. 2.

Chapter X.--Exhortation to the practice of virtue. [391]

Stand fast, therefore, in these things, and follow the example of the Lord, being firm and unchangeable in the faith, loving the brotherhood, [392] and being attached to one another, joined together in the truth, exhibiting the meekness of the Lord in your intercourse with one another, and despising no one. When you can do good, defer it not, because "alms delivers from death." [393] Be all of you subject one to another [394] "having your conduct blameless among the Gentiles," [395] that ye may both receive praise for your good works, and the Lord may not be blasphemed through you. But woe to him by whom the name of the Lord is blasphemed! [396] Teach, therefore, sobriety to all, and manifest it also in your own conduct.

[391] This and the two following chapters are preserved only in a Latin version. [See Jacobson, ad loc.]

[392] Comp. 1 Pet. ii. 17.

[393] Tobit iv. 10, Tobit xii. 9.

[394] Comp. 1 Pet. v. 5.

[395] 1 Pet. ii. 12.

[396] Isa. lii. 5.

Chapter XI.--Expression of grief on account of Valens.

I am greatly grieved for Valens, who was once a presbyter among you, because he so little understands the place that was given him [in the Church]. I exhort you, therefore, that ye abstain from covetousness, [397] and that ye be chaste and truthful. "Abstain from every form of evil." [398] For if a man cannot govern himself in such matters, how shall he enjoin them on others? If a man does not keep himself from covetousness, [399] he shall be defiled by idolatry, and shall be judged as one of the heathen. But who of us are ignorant of the judgment of the Lord? "Do we not know that the saints shall judge the world?" [400] as Paul teaches. But I have neither seen nor heard of any such thing among you, in the midst of whom the blessed Paul laboured, and who are commended [401] in the beginning of his Epistle. For he boasts of you in all those Churches which alone then knew the Lord; but we [of Smyrna] had not yet known Him. I am deeply grieved, therefore, brethren, for him (Valens) and his wife; to whom may the Lord grant true repentance! And be ye then moderate in regard to this matter, and "do not count such as enemies," [402] but call them back as suffering and straying members, that ye may save your whole body. For by so acting ye shall edify yourselves. [403]

[397] Some think that incontinence on the part of the Valens and his wife is referred to. [For many reasons I am glad the translators have preferred the reading pleonexias. The next word, chaste, sufficiently rebukes the example of Valens. For once I venture not to coincide with Jacobson's comment.]

[398] 1 Thess. v. 22.

[399] Some think that incontinence on the part of the Valens and his wife is referred to. [For many reasons I am glad the translators have preferred the reading pleonexias. The next word, chaste, sufficiently rebukes the example of Valens. For once I venture not to coincide with Jacobson's comment.]

[400] 1 Cor. vi. 2.

[401] Some read, "named;" comp. Phil. i. 5.

[402] 2 Thess. iii. 15.

[403] Comp. 1 Cor. xii. 26.

Chapter XII.--Exhortation to various graces.

For I trust that ye are well versed in the Sacred Scriptures, and that nothing is hid from you; but to me this privilege is not yet granted. [404] It is declared then in these Scriptures,

"Be ye angry, and sin not," [405] and, "Let not the sun go down upon your wrath." [406] Happy is he who remembers [407] this, which I believe to be the case with you. But may the God and Father of our Lord Jesus Christ, and Jesus Christ Himself, who is the Son of God, and our everlasting High Priest, build you up in faith and truth, and in all meekness, gentleness, patience, long-suffering, forbearance, and purity; and may He bestow on you a lot and portion among His saints, and on us with you, and on all that are under heaven, who shall believe in our Lord Jesus Christ, and in His Father, who "raised Him from the dead." [408] Pray for all the saints. Pray also for kings, [409] and potentates, and princes, and for those that persecute and hate you, [410] and for the enemies of the cross, that your fruit may be manifest to all, and that ye may be perfect in Him.

 [404] This passage is very obscure. Some render it as follows: "But at present it is not granted unto me to practise that which is written, Be ye angry," etc.

[405] Ps. iv. 5.

[406] Eph. iv. 26.

[407] Some read, "believes."

[408] Gal. i. 1.

[409] Comp. 1 Tim. ii. 2.

[410] Matt. v. 44.

Chapter XIII.--Concerning the transmission of epistles.

Both you and Ignatius [411] wrote to me, that if any one went [from this] into Syria, he should carry your letter [412] with him; which request I will attend to if I find a fitting opportunity, either personally, or through some other acting for me, that your desire may be fulfilled. The Epistles of Ignatius written by him [413] to us, and all the rest [of his Epistles] which we have by us, we have sent to you, as you requested. They are subjoined to this Epistle, and by them ye may be greatly profited; for they treat of faith and patience, and all things that tend to edification in our Lord. Any [414] more certain information you may have obtained respecting both Ignatius himself, and those that were [415] with him, have the goodness to make known [416] to us.

[411] Comp. Ep. of Ignatius to Polycarp, chap. viii.

[412] Or, "letters."

[413] Reference is here made to the two letters of Ignatius, one to Polycarp himself, and the other to the church at Smyrna.

[414] Henceforth, to the end, we have only the Latin version.

[415] The Latin version reads "are," which has been corrected as above.

[416] Polycarp was aware of the death of Ignatius (chap. ix.), but was as yet apparently ignorant of the circumstances attending it. [Who can fail to be touched by these affectionate yet entirely calm expressions as to his martyred

friend and brother? Martyrdom was the habitual end of Christ's soldiers, and Polycarp expected his own; hence his restrained and temperate words of interest.]

Chapter XIV.--Conclusion.

These things I have written to you by Crescens, whom up to the present [417] time I have recommended unto you, and do now recommend. For he has acted blamelessly among us, and I believe also among you. Moreover, ye will hold his sister in esteem when she comes to you. Be ye safe in the Lord Jesus Christ. Grace be with you all. [418] Amen.

[417] Some read, "in this present Epistle."

[418] Others read, "and in favour with all yours."

[337] The title of this Epistle in most of the mss. is, "The Epistle of St. Polycarp, Bishop of Smyrna, and holy martyr, to the Philippians."

[338] Or, "Polycarp, and those who with him are presbyters."

Introductory Note to the Epistle Concerning the Martyrdom of Polycarp

Internal evidence goes far to establish the credit which Eusebius lends to this specimen of the martyrologies, certainly not the earliest if we accept that of Ignatius as genuine. As an encyclical of one of "the seven churches" to another of the same Seven, and as bearing witness to their aggregation with others into the unity of "the Holy and Catholic Church," it is a very interesting witness, not only to an article of the creed, but to the original meaning and acceptation of the same. More than this, it is evidence of the strength of Christ perfected in human weakness; and thus it affords us an assurance of grace equal to our day in every time of need. When I see in it, however, an example of what a noble army of martyrs, women and children included, suffered in those days "for the testimony of Jesus," and in order to hand down the knowledge of the Gospel to these boastful ages of our own, I confess myself edified by what I read, chiefly because I am humbled and abashed in comparing what a Christian used to be, with what a Christian is, in our times, even at his best estate.

That this Epistle has been interpolated can hardly be doubted, when we compare it with the unvarnished specimen, in Eusebius. As for the "fragrant smell" that came from the fire, many kinds of wood emit the like in burning; and, apart from Oriental warmth of colouring, there seems nothing incredible in the narrative if we except "the dove" (chap. xvi.), which, however, is probably a corrupt reading, [419] as suggested by our translators. The blade was thrust into the martyr's left side; and this, opening the heart, caused the outpouring of a flood, and not a mere trickling. But, though Greek thus amended is a plausible conjecture, there seems to have been nothing of the kind in the copy quoted by Eusebius. On the other hand, note the truly catholic and scriptural testimony: "We love the martyrs, but the Son of God we worship: it is impossible for us to worship any other."

Bishop Jacobson assigns more than fifty pages to this martyrology, with a Latin version and abundant notes. To these I must refer the student, who may wish to see this attractive history in all the light of critical scholarship and, often, of admirable comment.

The following is the original Introductory Notice:--

The following letter purports to have been written by the Church at Smyrna to the Church at Philomelium, and through that Church to the whole Christian world, in order to give a succinct account of the circumstances attending the martyrdom of Polycarp. It is the earliest of all the Martyria, and has generally been accounted both the most interesting and authentic. Not a few, however, deem it interpolated in several passages, and some refer it to a much later date than the middle of the second century, to which it has been commonly ascribed. We cannot tell how much it may owe to the writers (chap. xxii.) who successively transcribed it. Great part of it has been engrossed by Eusebius in his Ecclesiastical History (iv. 15); and it is instructive to observe, that some of the most startling miraculous phenomena recorded in the text as it now stands, have no place in the narrative as given by that early historian of the Church. Much discussion has arisen respecting several particulars contained in this Martyrium; but into these disputes we do not enter, having it for our aim simply to present the reader with as faithful a translation as possible of this very interesting monument of Christian antiquity.

[419] See an ingenious conjecture in Bishop Wordsworth's Hippolytus and the Church of Rome, p. 318, C.

The Encyclical Epistle of the Church at Smyrna Concerning the Martyrdom of the Holy Polycarp

The Church of God which sojourns at Smyrna, to the Church of God sojourning in Philomelium, [420] and to all the congregations [421] of the Holy and Catholic Church in every place: Mercy, peace, and love from God the Father, and our Lord Jesus Christ, be multiplied.

Chapter I.--Subject of which we write.

We have written to you, brethren, as to what relates to the martyrs, and especially to the blessed Polycarp, who put an end to the persecution, having, as it were, set a seal upon it by his martyrdom. For almost all the events that happened previously [to this one], took place that the Lord might show us from above a martyrdom becoming the Gospel. For he waited to be delivered up, even as the Lord had done, that we also might become his followers, while we look not merely at what concerns ourselves but have regard also to our neighbours. For it is the part of a true and well-founded love, not only to wish one's self to be saved, but also all the brethren.

Chapter II.--The wonderful constancy of the martyrs.

All the martyrdoms, then, were blessed and noble which took place according to the will of God. For it becomes us who profess [422] greater piety than others, to ascribe the authority over all things to God. And truly, [423] who can fail to admire their nobleness of mind, and their patience, with that love towards their Lord which they displayed?-- who, when they were so torn with scourges, that the frame of their bodies, even to the very inward veins and arteries, was laid open, still patiently endured, while even those that stood by pitied and bewailed them. But they reached such a pitch of magnanimity, that not one of them let a sigh or a groan escape them; thus proving to us all that those holy martyrs of Christ, at the very time when they suffered such torments, were absent from the body, or rather, that the Lord then stood by them, and communed with them. And, looking to the grace of Christ, they despised all the torments of this world, redeeming themselves from eternal punishment by [the suffering of] a single hour. For this reason the fire of their savage executioners appeared cool to them. For they kept before their view escape from that fire which is eternal and never shall be quenched, and looked forward with the eyes of their heart to those good things which are laid up for such as endure; things "which ear hath not heard, nor eye seen, neither have entered into the heart of man," [424] but were revealed by the Lord to them, inasmuch as they were no longer men, but had already become angels. And, in like manner, those who were condemned to the wild beasts endured dreadful tortures, being stretched out upon beds full of spikes, and subjected to various other kinds of torments, in order that, if it were possible, the tyrant might, by their lingering tortures, lead them to a denial [of Christ].

[422] Literally, "who are more pious."

[423] The account now returns to the illustration of the statement made in the first sentence.

[424] 1 Cor. ii. 9.

Chapter III.--The constancy of Germanicus. The death of Polycarp is demanded.

For the devil did indeed invent many things against them; but thanks be to God, he could not prevail over all. For the most noble Germanicus strengthened the timidity of others by his own patience, and fought heroically [425] with the wild beasts. For, when the proconsul sought to persuade him, and urged him [426] to take pity upon his age, he attracted the wild beast towards himself, and provoked it, being desirous to escape all the more quickly from an unrighteous and impious world. But upon this the whole multitude, marvelling at the nobility of mind displayed by the devout and godly race of Christians, [427] cried out, "Away with the Atheists; let Polycarp be sought out!"

[425] Or, "illustriously."

[426] Or, "said to him."

[427] Literally, "the nobleness of the God-loving and God-fearing race of Christians."

Chapter IV.--Quintus the apostate.

Now one named Quintus, a Phrygian, who was but lately come from Phrygia, when he saw the wild beasts, became afraid. This was the man who forced himself and some others to come forward voluntarily [for trial]. Him the proconsul, after many entreaties, persuaded to swear and to offer sacrifice. Wherefore, brethren, we do not commend those who give themselves up [to suffering], seeing the Gospel does not teach so to do. [428]

[428] Comp. Matt. x. 23.

Chapter V.--The departure and vision of Polycarp.

But the most admirable Polycarp, when he first heard [that he was sought for], was in no measure disturbed, but resolved to continue in the city. However, in deference to the wish of many, he was persuaded to leave it. He departed, therefore, to a country house not far distant from the city. There he stayed with a few [friends], engaged in nothing else night and day than praying for all men, and for the Churches throughout the world, according to his usual custom. And while he was praying, a vision presented itself to him three days before he was taken; and, behold, the pillow under his head seemed to him on fire. Upon this, turning to those that were with him, he said to them prophetically, "I must be burnt alive."

Chapter VI.--Polycarp is betrayed by a servant.

And when those who sought for him were at hand, he departed to another dwelling, whither his pursuers immediately came after him. And when they found him not, they seized upon two youths [that were there], one of whom, being subjected to torture, confessed. It was thus impossible that he should continue hid, since those that betrayed him were of his own household. The Irenarch [429] then (whose office is the same as that of the Cleronomus [430]), by name Herod, hastened to bring him into the stadium. [This all happened] that he might fulfil his special lot, being made a partaker of Christ, and that they who betrayed him might undergo the punishment of Judas himself.

[429] It was the duty of the Irenarch to apprehend all seditious troublers of the public peace.

[430] Some think that those magistrates bore this name that were elected by lot.

Chapter VII.--Polycarp is found by his pursuers.

His pursuers then, along with horsemen, and taking the youth with them, went forth at supper-time on the day of the preparation [431] with their usual weapons, as if going out against a robber. [432] And being come about evening [to the place where he was], they found him lying down in the upper room of [433] a certain little house, from which he might have escaped into another place; but he refused, saying, "The will of God [434] be done." [435] So when he heard that they were come, he went down and spake with them. And as those that were present marvelled at his age and constancy, some of them said. "Was so much effort [436] made to capture such a venerable man?" [437] Immediately then, in that very hour, he ordered that something to eat and drink should be set before them, as much indeed as they cared for, while he besought them to allow him an hour to pray without disturbance. And on their giving him leave, he stood and prayed, being full of the grace of God, so that he could not cease [438] for two full hours, to the astonishment of them that heard him, insomuch that many began to repent that they had come forth against so godly and venerable an old man.

[431] That is, on Friday.

[432] Comp. Matt. xxvi. 55.

[433] Or, "in."

[434] Some read "the Lord"

[435] Comp. Matt. vi. 10; Acts xxi. 14.

[436] Or, "diligence."

[437] Jacobson reads, "and [marvelling] that they had used so great diligence to capture," etc.

[438] Or, "be silent."

Chapter VIII.--Polycarp is brought into the city.

Now, as soon as he had ceased praying, having made mention of all that had at any time come in contact with him, both small and great, illustrious and obscure, as well as the whole Catholic Church throughout the world, the time of his departure having arrived, they set him upon an ass, and conducted him into the city, the day being that of the great Sabbath. And the Irenarch Herod, accompanied by his father Nicetes (both riding in a chariot [439]), met him, and taking him up into the chariot, they seated themselves beside him, and endeavoured to persuade him, saying, "What harm is there in saying, Lord Cæsar, [440] and in sacrificing, with the other ceremonies observed on such occasions, and so make sure of safety?" But he at first gave them no answer; and when they continued to urge him, he said, "I shall not do as you advise me." So they, having no hope of persuading him, began to speak bitter [441] words unto him, and cast him with violence out of the chariot, [442] insomuch that, in getting down from the carriage, he dislocated his leg [443] [by the fall]. But without being disturbed, [444] and as if suffering nothing, he went eagerly forward with all haste, and was conducted to the stadium, where the tumult was so great, that there was no possibility of being heard.

[439] Jacobson deems these words an interpolation.

[440] Or, "Cæsar is Lord," all the mss. having kurios instead of kurie, as usually printed.

[441] Or, "terrible."

[442] Or, "cast him down" simply, the following words being, as above, an interpolation.

[443] Or, "sprained his ankle."

[444] Or, "not turning back."

Chapter IX.--Polycarp refuses to revile Christ.

Now, as Polycarp was entering into the stadium, there came to him a voice from heaven, saying, "Be strong, and show thyself a man, O Polycarp!" No one saw who it was that spoke to him; but those of our brethren who were present heard the voice. And as he was brought forward, the tumult became great when they heard that Polycarp was taken. And when he came near, the proconsul asked him whether he was Polycarp. On his confessing that he was, [the proconsul] sought to persuade him to deny [Christ], saying, "Have respect to thy old age," and other similar things, according to their custom, [such as], "Swear by the fortune of Cæsar; repent, and say, Away with the Atheists." But Polycarp, gazing with a stern countenance on all the multitude of the wicked heathen then in the stadium, and waving his hand towards them, while with groans he looked up to heaven, said, "Away with the Atheists." [445] Then, the proconsul urging him, and saying, "Swear, and I will set thee at liberty, reproach Christ;" Polycarp declared, "Eighty and six years have I served Him, and He never did me any injury: how then can I blaspheme my King and my Saviour?"

[445] Referring the words to the heathen, and not to the Christians, as was desired.

Chapter X.--Polycarp confesses himself a Christian.

And when the proconsul yet again pressed him, and said, "Swear by the fortune of Cæsar," he answered, "Since thou art vainly urgent that, as thou sayest, I should swear by the fortune of Cæsar, and pretendest not to know who and what I am, hear me declare with boldness, I am a Christian. And if you wish to learn what the doctrines [446] of Christianity are, appoint me a day, and thou shalt hear them." The proconsul replied, "Persuade the people." But Polycarp said, "To thee I have thought it right to offer an account [of my faith]; for we are taught to give all due honour (which entails no injury upon ourselves) to the powers and authorities which are ordained of God. [447] But as for these, I do not deem them worthy of receiving any account from me." [448]

[446] Or, "an account of Christianity."

[447] Comp. Rom. xiii. 1-7; Tit. iii. 1.

[448] Or, "of my making any defence to them."

Chapter XI.--No threats have any effect on Polycarp.

The proconsul then said to him, "I have wild beasts at hand; to these will I cast thee, except thou repent." But he answered, "Call them then, for we are not accustomed to repent of what is good in order to adopt that which is evil; [449] and it is well for me to be changed from what is evil to what is righteous." [450] But again the proconsul said to him, "I will cause thee to be consumed by fire, seeing thou despisest the wild beasts, if thou wilt not repent." But Polycarp said, "Thou threatenest me with fire which burneth for an hour, and after a little is extinguished, but art ignorant of the fire of the coming judgment and of eternal punishment, reserved for the ungodly. But why tarriest thou? Bring forth what thou wilt."

[449] Literally, "repentance from things better to things worse is a change impossible to us."

[450] That is, to leave this world for a better.

Chapter XII.--Polycarp is sentenced to be burned.

While he spoke these and many other like things, he was filled with confidence and joy, and his countenance was full of grace, so that not merely did it not fall as if troubled by the things said to him, but, on the contrary, the proconsul was astonished, and sent his herald to proclaim in the midst of the stadium thrice, "Polycarp has confessed that he is a Christian." This proclamation having been made by the herald, the whole multitude both of the heathen and Jews, who dwelt at Smyrna, cried out with uncontrollable fury, and in a loud voice, "This is the teacher of Asia, [451] the father of the Christians, and the overthrower of our gods, he who has been teaching many not to sacrifice, or to worship the gods." Speaking thus, they cried out, and besought Philip the Asiarch [452] to let loose a lion upon Polycarp. But Philip answered that it was not lawful for him to do so, seeing the shows [453] of wild beasts were already finished. Then it seemed good to them to cry out with one consent, that Polycarp should be burnt alive. For thus it behooved the vision which was revealed to him in regard to his pillow to be fulfilled, when, seeing it on fire as he was praying, he turned about and said prophetically to the faithful that were with him, "I must be burnt alive."

 [451] Some read, "ungodliness," but the above seems preferable.

[452] The Asiarchs were those who superintended all arrangements connected with the games in the several provinces.

[453] Literally, "the baiting of dogs."

Chapter XIII.--The funeral pile is erected.

This, then, was carried into effect with greater speed than it was spoken, the multitudes immediately gathering together wood and fagots out of the shops and baths; the Jews especially, according to custom, eagerly assisting them in it. And when the funeral pile was ready, Polycarp, laying aside all his garments, and loosing his girdle, sought also to take off his sandals,--a thing he was not accustomed to do, inasmuch as every one of the faithful was always eager who should first touch his skin. For, on account of his holy life, [454] he was, even before his martyrdom, adorned [455] with every kind of good. Immediately then they surrounded him with those substances which had been prepared for the funeral pile. But when they were about also to fix him with nails, he said, "Leave me as I am; for He that giveth me strength to endure the fire, will also enable me, without your securing me by nails, to remain without moving in the pile."

[454] Literally, "good behaviour."

[455] Some think this implies that Polycarp's skin was believed to possess a miraculous efficacy.

Chapter XIV.--The prayer of Polycarp.

They did not nail him then, but simply bound him. And he, placing his hands behind him, and being bound like a distinguished ram [taken] out of a great flock for sacrifice, and prepared to be an acceptable burnt-offering unto God, looked up to heaven, and said, "O Lord God Almighty, the Father of thy beloved and blessed Son Jesus Christ, by whom we have received the knowledge of Thee, the God of angels and powers, and of every creature, and of the whole race of the righteous who live before thee, I give Thee thanks that Thou hast counted me worthy of this day and this hour, that I should have a part in the number of Thy martyrs, in the cup [456] of thy Christ, to the resurrection of eternal life, both of soul and body, through the incorruption [imparted] by the Holy Ghost. Among whom may I be accepted this day before Thee as a fat [457] and acceptable sacrifice, according as Thou, the ever-truthful [458] God, hast foreordained, hast revealed beforehand to me, and now hast fulfilled. Wherefore also I praise Thee for all things, I bless Thee, I glorify Thee, along with the everlasting and heavenly Jesus Christ, Thy beloved Son, with whom, to Thee, and the Holy Ghost, be glory both now and to all coming ages. Amen." [459]

[456] Comp. Matt. xx. 22, Matt. xxvi. 39; Mark x. 38.

[457] Literally, "in a fat," etc., [or, "in a rich"].

[458] Literally, "the not false and true God."

[459] Eusebius (Hist. Eccl., iv. 15) has preserved a great portion of this Martyrium, but in a text considerably differing from that we have followed. Here, instead of "and," he has "in the Holy Ghost."

Chapter XV.--Polycarp is not injured by the fire.

When he had pronounced this amen, and so finished his prayer, those who were appointed for the purpose kindled the fire. And as the flame blazed forth in great fury, [460] we, to whom it was given to witness it, beheld a great miracle, and have been preserved that we might report to others what then took place. For the fire, shaping itself into the form of an arch, like the sail of a ship when filled with the wind, encompassed as by a circle the body of the martyr. And he appeared within not like flesh which is burnt, but as bread that is baked, or as gold and silver glowing in a furnace. Moreover, we perceived such a sweet odour [coming from the pile], as if frankincense or some such precious spices had been smoking [461] there.

[460] Literally, "a great flame shining forth."

[461] Literally, "breathing."

Chapter XVI.--Polycarp is pierced by a dagger.

At length, when those wicked men perceived that his body could not be consumed by the fire, they commanded an executioner to go near and pierce him through with a dagger. And on his doing this, there came forth a dove, [462] and a great quantity of blood, so that the fire was extinguished; and all the people wondered that there should be such a difference between the unbelievers and the elect, of whom this most admirable Polycarp was one, having in our own times been an apostolic and prophetic teacher, and bishop of the Catholic Church which is in Smyrna. For every word that went out of his mouth either has been or shall yet be accomplished.

[462] Eusebius omits all mention of the dove, and many have thought the text to be here corrupt. It has been proposed to read ep' aristera, "on the left hand side," instead of peristera, "a dove."

Chapter XVII.--The Christians are refused Polycarp's body.

But when the adversary of the race of the righteous, the envious, malicious, and wicked one, perceived the impressive [463] nature of his martyrdom, and [considered] the blameless life he had led from the beginning, and how he was now crowned with the wreath of immortality, having beyond dispute received his reward, he did his utmost that not the least memorial of him should be taken away by us, although many desired to do this, and to become possessors [464] of his holy flesh. For this end he suggested it to Nicetes, the father of Herod and brother of Alce, to go and entreat the governor not to give up his body to be buried, "lest," said he, "forsaking Him that was crucified, they begin to worship this one." This he said at the suggestion and urgent persuasion of the Jews, who also watched us, as we sought to take him out of the fire, being ignorant of this, that it is neither possible for us ever to forsake Christ, who suffered for the salvation of such as shall be saved throughout the whole world (the blameless one for sinners [465]), nor to worship any other. For Him indeed, as being the Son of God, we adore; but the martyrs, as disciples and followers of the Lord, we worthily love on account of their extraordinary [466] affection towards their own King and Master, of whom may we also be made companions [467] and fellow-disciples!

[463] Literally, "greatness."

[464] The Greek, literally translated, is, "and to have fellowship with his holy flesh."

[465] This clause is omitted by Eusebius: it was probably interpolated by some transcriber, who had in his mind 1 Pet. iii. 18.

[466] Literally, "unsurpassable."

[467] Literally, "fellow-partakers."

Chapter XVIII.--The body of Polycarp is burned.

The centurion then, seeing the strife excited by the Jews, placed the body [468] in the midst of the fire, and consumed it. Accordingly, we afterwards took up his bones, as being more precious than the most exquisite jewels, and more purified [469] than gold, and deposited them in a fitting place, whither, being gathered together, as opportunity is allowed us, with joy and rejoicing, the Lord shall grant us to celebrate the anniversary [470] of his martyrdom, both in memory of those who have already finished their course, [471] and for the exercising and preparation of those yet to walk in their steps.

[468] Or, "him."

[469] Or, "more tried."

[470] Literally, "the birth-day."

[471] Literally, "been athletes."

Chapter XIX.--Praise of the martyr Polycarp.

This, then, is the account of the blessed Polycarp, who, being the twelfth that was martyred in Smyrna (reckoning those also of Philadelphia), yet occupies a place of his own [472] in the memory of all men, insomuch that he is everywhere spoken of by the heathen themselves. He was not merely an illustrious teacher, but also a pre-eminent martyr, whose martyrdom all desire to imitate, as having been altogether consistent with the Gospel of Christ. For, having through patience overcome the unjust governor, and thus acquired the crown of immortality, he now, with the apostles and all the righteous [in heaven], rejoicingly glorifies God, even the Father, and blesses our Lord Jesus Christ, the Saviour of our souls, the Governor of our bodies, and the Shepherd of the Catholic Church throughout the world. [473]

[472] Literally, "is alone remembered."

[473] Several additions are here made. One ms. has, "and the all-holy and life-giving Spirit;" while the old Latin version reads, "and the Holy Spirit, by whom we know all things."

Chapter XX.--This epistle is to be transmitted to the brethren.

Since, then, ye requested that we would at large make you acquainted with what really took place, we have for the present sent you this summary account through our brother Marcus. When, therefore, ye have yourselves read this Epistle, [474] be pleased to send it to the brethren at a greater distance, that they also may glorify the Lord, who makes such choice of His own servants. To Him who is able to bring us all by His grace and goodness [475] into his everlasting kingdom, through His only-begotten Son Jesus Christ, to Him be glory, and honour, and power, and majesty, for ever. Amen. Salute all the saints. They that are with us salute you, and Evarestus, who wrote this Epistle, with all his house.

[474] Literally, "having learned these things."

[475] Literally, "gift."

Chapter XXI.--The date of the martyrdom.

Now, the blessed Polycarp suffered martyrdom on the second day of the month Xanthicus just begun, [476] the seventh day before the Kalends of May, on the great Sabbath, at the eighth hour. [477] He was taken by Herod, Philip the Trallian being high priest, [478] Statius Quadratus being proconsul, but Jesus Christ being King for ever, to whom be glory, honour, majesty, and an everlasting throne, from generation to generation. Amen.

 [476] The translation is here very doubtful. Wake renders the words menos histamenou, "of the present month."

[477] Great obscurity hangs over the chronology here indicated. According to Usher, the Smyrnæans began the month Xanthicus on the 25th of March. But the seventh day before the Kalends of May is the 25th of April. Some, therefore, read 'Aprillion instead of Maion. The great Sabbath is that before the passover. The "eighth hour" may correspond either to our 8 a.m. or 2 p.m.

[478] Called before (chap. xii.) Asiarch.

Chapter XXII.--Salutation.

We wish you, brethren, all happiness, while you walk according to the doctrine of the Gospel of Jesus Christ; with whom be glory to God the Father and the Holy Spirit, for the salvation of His holy elect, after whose example

[479] the blessed Polycarp suffered, following in whose steps may we too be found in the kingdom of Jesus Christ!

These things [480] Caius transcribed from the copy of Irenæus (who was a disciple of Polycarp), having himself been intimate with Irenæus. And I Socrates transcribed them at Corinth from the copy of Caius. Grace be with you all.

And I again, Pionius, wrote them from the previously written copy, having carefully searched into them, and the blessed Polycarp having manifested them to me through a revelation, even as I shall show in what follows. I have collected these things, when they had almost faded away through the lapse of time, that the Lord Jesus Christ may also gather me along with His elect into His heavenly kingdom, to whom, with the Father and the Holy Spirit, be glory for ever and ever. Amen.

[479] Literally, "according as."

[480] What follows is, of course, no part of the original Epistle.

[420] Some read, "Philadelphia," but on inferior authority. Philomelium was a city of Phrygia.

[421] The word in the original is poroikiais, from which the English "parishes" is derived.

Barnabas

Introductory Note to the Epistle of Barnabas

[a.d. 100.] The writer of this Epistle is supposed to have been an Alexandrian Jew of the times of Trajan and Hadrian. He was a layman; but possibly he bore the name of "Barnabas," and so has been confounded with his holy and apostolic name-sire. It is more probable that the Epistle, being anonymous, was attributed to St. Barnabas, by those who supposed that apostle to be the author of the Epistle to the Hebrews, and who discovered similarities in the plan and purpose of the two works. It is with great reluctance that I yield to modern scholars, in dismissing the ingenious and temperate argument of Archbishop Wake [1438] for the apostolic origin of this treatise. The learned Lardner [1439] shares his convictions; and the very interesting and ingenious views of Jones [1440] never appeared to me satisfactory, weighed with preponderating arguments, on the other side. [1441]

The Maccabæan spirit of the Jews never burned more furiously than after the destruction of Jerusalem, and while it was kindling the conflagration that broke out under Barchochebas, and blazed so terribly in the insurrection against Hadrian. [1442] It is not credible that the Jewish Christians at Alexandria and elsewhere were able to emancipate themselves from their national spirit; and accordingly the old Judaizing, which St. Paul had anathematized and confuted, would assert itself again. If such was the occasion of this Epistle, as I venture to suppose, a higher character must be ascribed to it than could otherwise be claimed. This accounts, also, for the degree of favour with which it was accepted by the primitive faithful.

It is interesting as a specimen of their conflicts with a persistent Judaism which St. Paul had defeated and anathematized, but which was ever cropping out among believers originally of the Hebrews. [1443] Their own habits of allegorizing, and their Oriental tastes, must be borne in mind, if we are readily disgusted with our author's fancies and refinements. St. Paul himself pays a practical tribute to their modes of thought, in his Epistle to the Galatians iv. 24. This is the ad hominem form of rhetoric, familiar to all speakers, which laid even the apostle open to the slander of enemies (2 Cor. xii. 16),--that he was "crafty," and caught men with guile. It is interesting to note the more Occidental spirit of Cyprian, as compared with our author, when he also contends with Judaism. Doubtless we have in the pseudo-Barnabas something of that oeconomy which is always capable of abuse, and which was destined too soon to overleap the bounds of its moral limitations.

It is to be observed that this writer sometimes speaks as a Gentile, a fact which some have found it difficult to account for, on the supposition that he was a Hebrew, if not a Levite as well. But so, also, St. Paul sometimes speaks as a Roman, and sometimes as a Jew; and, owing to the mixed character of the early Church, he writes to the Romans iv. 1 as if they were all Israelites, and again to the same Church (Rom. xi. 13) as if they were all Gentiles. So this writer sometimes identifies himself with Jewish thought as a son of Abraham, and again speaks from the Christian position as if he were a Gentile, thus identifying himself with the catholicity of the Church.

But the subject thus opened is vast; and "the Epistle of Barnabas," so called, still awaits a critical editor, who at the same time shall be a competent expositor. Nobody can answer these requisitions, who is unable, for this purpose, to be a Christian of the days of Trajan.

But it will be observed that this version has great advantages over any of its predecessor, and is a valuable acquisition to the student. The learned translators have had before them the entire Greek text of the fourth century, disfigured it is true by corruptions, but still very precious, the rather as they have been able to compare it with the text of Hilgenfeld. Their editorial notes are sufficient for our own plan; and little has been left for me to do, according to the scheme of this publication, save to revise the "copy" for printing. I am glad to presume no further into such a labyrinth, concerning which the learned and careful Wake modestly professes, "I have endeavoured to attain to the sense of my author, and to make him as plain and easy as I was able. If in anything I have chanced to mistake him, I have only this to say for myself: that he must be better acquainted with the road than I pretend to be, who will undertake to travel so long a journey in the dark and never to miss his way."

The following is the original Introductory Notice:--

Nothing certain is known as to the author of the following Epistle. The writer's name is Barnabas, but scarcely any scholars now ascribe it to the illustrious friend and companion of St. Paul. External and internal evidence here come into direct collision. The ancient writers who refer to this Epistle unanimously attribute it to Barnabas the Levite, of Cyprus, who held such an honourable place in the infant Church. Clement of Alexandria does so again and again (Strom., ii. 6, ii. 7, etc.). Origen describes it as "a Catholic Epistle" (Cont. Cels., i. 63), and seems to rank it among the Sacred Scriptures (Comm. in Rom., i. 24). Other statements have been quoted from the fathers, to show that they held this to be an authentic production of the apostolic Barnabas; and certainly no other name is ever hinted at in Christian antiquity as that of the writer. But notwithstanding this, the internal evidence is now generally regarded as conclusive against this opinion. On perusing the Epistle, the reader will be in circumstances to judge of this matter for himself. He will be led to consider whether the spirit and tone of the writing, as so decidedly opposed to all respect for Judaism--the numerous inaccuracies which it contains with respect to Mosaic enactments and observances --the absurd and trifling interpretations of Scripture which it suggests--and the many silly vaunts of superior knowledge in which its writer indulges--can possibly comport with its ascription to the fellow--labourer of St. Paul. When it is remembered that no one ascribes the Epistle to the apostolic Barnabas till the times of Clement of Alexandria, and that it is ranked by Eusebius among the "spurious" writings, which, however much known and read in the Church, were never regarded as authoritative, little doubt can remain that the external evidence is of itself weak, and should not make us hesitate for a moment in refusing to ascribe this writing to Barnabas the Apostle.

The date, object, and intended reader of the Epistle can only be doubtfully inferred from some statements which it contains. It was clearly written after the destruction of Jerusalem, since reference is made to that event (chap. xvi.), but how long after is matter of much dispute. The general opinion is, that its date is not later than the middle of the second century, and that it cannot be placed earlier than some twenty or thirty years before. In point of style, both as respects thought and expression, a very low place must be assigned it. We know nothing certain of the region in which the author lived, or where the first readers were to be found. The intention of the writer, as he himself states (chap. i), was "to perfect the knowledge" of those to whom he wrote. Hilgenfeld, who has devoted much attention to this Epistle, holds that "it was written at the close of the first century by a Gentile Christian of the school of Alexandria, with the view of winning back, or guarding from a Judaic form of Christianity, those Christians belonging to the same class as himself."

Until the recent discovery of the Codex Sinaiticus by Tischendorf, the first four and a half chapters were known only in an ancient Latin version. The whole Greek text is now happily recovered, though it is in many places very corrupt. We have compared its readings throughout, and noted the principal variations from the text represented in our version. We have also made frequent reference to the text adopted by Hilgenfeld in his recent edition of the Epistle (Lipsiæ, T. O. Weigel, 1886).

[1438] Discourse (p. 148) to his Genuine Epistles of the Apostolical Fathers. Philadelphia, 1846.

[1439] Works, ii. 250, note; and iv. 128.

[1440] On the Canon, vol. ii. p. 431.

[1441] To those who may adhere to the older opinion, let me commend the eloquent and instructive chapter (xxiii.) in Farrar's Life of St. Paul.

[1442] Hadrian's purpose to rebuild their city seems to be pointed out in chap. xvi.

[1443] M. Renan may be read with pain, and yet with profit, in much that his Gallio-spirit suggests on this subject. Chap. v., St. Paul, Paris, 1884.

The Epistle of Barnabas [1444]

Chapter I.--After the salutation, the writer declares that he would communicate to his brethren something of that which he had himself received.

All hail, ye sons and daughters, in the name of our Lord [1445] Jesus Christ, who loved us in peace.

Seeing that the divine fruits [1446] of righteousness abound among you, I rejoice exceedingly and above measure in your happy and honoured spirits, because ye have with such effect received the engrafted [1447] spiritual gift. Wherefore also I inwardly rejoice the more, hoping to be saved, because I truly perceive in you the Spirit poured forth from the rich Lord [1448] of love. Your greatly desired appearance has thus filled me with astonishment over you. [1449] I am therefore persuaded of this, and fully convinced in my own mind, that since I began to speak among you I understand many things, because the Lord hath accompanied me in the way of righteousness. I am also on this account bound [1450] by the strictest obligation to love you above my own soul, because great are the faith and love dwelling in you, while you hope for the life which He has promised. [1451] Considering this, therefore, that if I should take the trouble to communicate to you some portion of what I have myself received, it will prove to me a sufficient reward that I minister to such spirits, I have hastened briefly to write unto you, in order that, along with your faith, ye might have perfect knowledge. The doctrines of the Lord, then, are three: [1452] the hope of life, the beginning and the completion of it. For the Lord hath made known to us by the prophets both the things which are past and present, giving us also the first-fruits of the knowledge [1453] of things to come, which things as we see accomplished, one by one, we ought with the greater richness of faith [1454] and elevation of spirit to draw near to Him with reverence. [1455] I then, not as your teacher, but as one of yourselves, will set forth a few things by which in present circumstances ye may be rendered the more joyful.

[1445] The Cod. Sin. has simply, "the Lord."

[1446] Literally, "the judgments of God being great and rich towards you;" but, as Hefele remarks, dikaioma seems here to have the meaning of righteousness, as in Rom. v. 18.

[1447] This appears to be the meaning of the Greek, and is confirmed by the ancient Latin version. Hilgenfeld, however, following Cod. Sin., reads "thus," instead of "because," and separates the clauses.

[1448] The Latin reads, "spirit infused into you from the honourable fountain of God."

[1449] This sentence is entirely omitted in the Latin.

[1450] The Latin text is here quite different, and seems evidently corrupt. We have followed the Cod. Sin., as does Hilgenfeld.

[1451] Literally, "in the hope of His life."

[1452] The Greek is here totally unintelligible: it seems impossible either to punctuate or construe it. We may attempt to represent it as follows: "The doctrines of the Lord, then, are three: Life, Faith, and Hope, our beginning and end; and Righteousness, the beginning and the end of judgment; Love and Joy and the Testimony of gladness for works of righteousness." We have followed the ancient Latin text, which Hilgenfeld also adopts, though Weitzäcker and others prefer the Greek.

[1453] Instead of "knowledge" (gnoseos), Cod. Sin. has "taste" (geuseos).

[1454] Literally, "we ought more richly and loftily to approach His fear."

[1455] Instead of, "to Him with fear," the reading of Cod. Sin., the Latin has, "to His altar," which Hilgenfeld adopts.

Chapter II.--The Jewish sacrifices are now abolished.

Since, therefore, the days are evil, and Satan [1456] possesses the power of this world, we ought to give heed to

ourselves, and diligently inquire into the ordinances of the
Lord. Fear and patience, then, are helpers of our faith; and
long-suffering and continence are things which fight on our
side. While these remain pure in what respects the Lord,
Wisdom, Understanding, Science, and Knowledge rejoice
along with them. [1457] For He hath revealed to us by all
the prophets that He needs neither sacrifices, nor burnt-
offerings, nor oblations, saying thus, "What is the multitude
of your sacrifices unto Me, saith the Lord? I am full of
burnt-offerings, and desire not the fat of lambs, and the
blood of bulls and goats, not when ye come to appear
before Me: for who hath required these things at your
hands? Tread no more My courts, not though ye bring with
you fine flour. Incense is a vain abomination unto Me, and
your new moons and sabbaths I cannot endure." [1458] He
has therefore abolished these things, that the new law of
our Lord Jesus Christ, which is without the yoke of
necessity, might have a human oblation. [1459] And again
He says to them, "Did I command your fathers, when they
went out from the land of Egypt, to offer unto Me burnt-
offerings and sacrifices? But this rather I commanded them,
Let no one of you cherish any evil in his heart against his
neighbour, and love not an oath of falsehood." [1460] We
ought therefore, being possessed of understanding, to
perceive the gracious intention of our Father; for He speaks
to us, desirous that we, not [1461] going astray like them,
should ask how we may approach Him. To us, then, He
declares, "A sacrifice [pleasing] to God is a broken spirit; a
smell of sweet savour to the Lord is a heart that glorifieth
Him that made it." [1462] We ought therefore, brethren,
carefully to inquire concerning our salvation, lest the wicked

one, having made his entrance by deceit, should hurl [1463] us forth from our [true] life.

[1456] The Latin text is literally, "the adversary;" the Greek has, "and he that worketh possesseth power;" Hilgenfeld reads, "he that worketh against," the idea expressed above being intended.

[1457] Or, "while these things continue, those which respect the Lord rejoice in purity along with them--Wisdom," etc.

[1458] Isa. i. 11-14, from the Sept., as is the case throughout. We have given the quotation as it stands in Cod. Sin.

[1459] Thus in the Latin. The Greek reads, "might not have a man-made oblation." The Latin text seems preferable, implying that, instead of the outward sacrifices of the law, there is now required a dedication of man himself. Hilgenfeld follows the Greek.

[1460] Jer. vii. 22; Zech. viii. 17.

[1461] So the Greek. Hilgenfeld, with the Latin, omits "not."

[1462] Ps. li. 19. There is nothing in Scripture corresponding to the last clause.

[1463] Literally, "sling us out."

Chapter III.--The fasts of the Jews are not true fasts, nor acceptable to God.

He says then to them again concerning these things, "Why do ye fast to Me as on this day, saith the Lord, that your voice should be heard with a cry? I have not chosen this fast, saith the Lord, that a man should humble his soul. Nor, though ye bend your neck like a ring, and put upon you sackcloth and ashes, will ye call it an acceptable fast." [1464] To us He saith, "Behold, this is the fast that I have chosen, saith the Lord, not that a man should humble his soul, but that he should loose every band of iniquity, untie the fastenings of harsh agreements, restore to liberty them that are bruised, tear in pieces every unjust engagement, feed the hungry with thy bread, clothe the naked when thou seest him, bring the homeless into thy house, not despise the humble if thou behold him, and not [turn away] from the members of thine own family. Then shall thy dawn break forth, and thy healing shall quickly spring up, and righteousness shall go forth before thee, and the glory of God shall encompass thee; and then thou shalt call, and God shall hear thee; whilst thou art yet speaking, He shall say, Behold, I am with thee; if thou take away from thee the chain [binding others], and the stretching forth of the hands [1465] [to swear falsely], and words of murmuring, and give cheerfully thy bread to the hungry, and show compassion to the soul that has been humbled." [1466] To this end, therefore, brethren, He is long-suffering, foreseeing how the people whom He has prepared shall with guilelessness believe in His Beloved. For He revealed all these things to us beforehand, that we should not rush forward as rash acceptors of their laws. [1467]

[1464] Isa. lviii. 4, 5.

[1465] The original here is cheirotonian, from the LXX. Hefele remarks, that it may refer to the stretching forth of the hands, either to swear falsely, or to mock and insult one's neighbour.

[1466] Isa. lviii. 6-10.

[1467] The Greek is here unintelligible: the Latin has, "that we should not rush on, as if proselytes to their law."

Chapter IV.--Antichrist is at hand: let us therefore avoid Jewish errors.

It therefore behoves us, who inquire much concerning events at hand, [1468] to search diligently into those things which are able to save us. Let us then utterly flee from all the works of iniquity, lest these should take hold of us; and let us hate the error of the present time, that we may set our love on the world to come: let us not give loose reins to our soul, that it should have power to run with sinners and the wicked, lest we become like them. The final stumbling-block (or source of danger) approaches, concerning which it is written, as Enoch [1469] says, "For for this end the Lord has cut short the times and the days, that His Beloved may hasten; and He will come to the inheritance." And the prophet also speaks thus: "Ten kingdoms shall reign upon the earth, and a little king shall rise up after them, who shall subdue under one three of the kings." [1470] In like manner Daniel says concerning the same, "And I beheld the fourth beast, wicked and powerful, and more savage than all the beasts of the earth, and how from it sprang up ten horns, and out of them a little budding horn, and how it subdued under one three of the great horns." [1471] Ye ought therefore to understand. And this also I further beg of you, as being one of you, and loving you both individually and collectively more than my own soul, to take heed now to yourselves, and not to be like some, adding largely to your sins, and saying, "The covenant is both theirs and ours." [1472] But they thus finally lost it, after Moses had already received it. For the Scripture saith, "And Moses was fasting in the mount forty days and forty nights, and received the covenant from the Lord, tables of stone written with the finger of the hand of the Lord;" [1473] but turning away to idols, they lost it. For the Lord speaks thus to Moses: "Moses go down quickly; for the people whom thou hast brought out of the land of Egypt have transgressed." [1474] And Moses understood [the meaning of God], and cast the two tables out of his hands; and their covenant was broken, in order that the covenant of the beloved Jesus might be sealed upon our heart, in the hope which flows from believing in Him. [1475] Now, being desirous to write many things to you, not as your teacher, but as becometh one who loves you, I have taken care not to fail to write to you from what I myself possess, with a view to your purification. [1476] We take earnest [1477] heed in these last days; for the whole [past] time of your faith will profit you nothing, unless now in this wicked time we also withstand coming sources of danger, as becometh the sons of God. That the Black One [1478] may find no means of entrance, let us flee from every vanity, let us utterly hate the works of the way of wickedness. Do not, by retiring apart, live a solitary life, as if you were already [fully] justified; but coming together in one place, make common inquiry concerning what tends to your general welfare. For the Scripture saith, "Woe to them who are wise to themselves, and prudent in their own sight!" [1479] Let us be spiritually-minded: let us be a perfect temple to God. As much as in us lies, let us meditate upon the fear of God, and let us keep His commandments, that we may rejoice in His ordinances. The Lord will judge the world without respect of persons. Each will receive as he has done: if he is righteous, his righteousness will precede him; if he is wicked, the reward of wickedness is before him. Take heed, lest resting at our ease, as those who are the called [of God], we should fall asleep in our sins, and the wicked prince, acquiring power over us, should thrust us away from the kingdom of the Lord. And all the more attend to this, my brethren, when ye reflect and behold, that after so great signs and wonders were wrought in Israel, they were thus [at length] abandoned. Let us beware lest we be found [fulfilling that saying], as it is written, "Many are called, but few are chosen." [1480]

[1468] Or it might be rendered, "things present." Cotelerius reads, "de his instantibus."

[1469] The Latin reads, "Daniel" instead of "Enoch;" comp. Dan. ix. 24-27.

[1470] Dan. vii. 24, very loosely quoted.

[1471] Dan. vii. 7, 8, also very inaccurately cited.

[1472] We here follow the Latin text in preference to the Greek, which reads merely, "the covenant is ours." What follows seems to show the correctness of the Latin, as the author proceeds to deny that the Jews had any further interest in the promises.

[1473] Ex. xxxi. 18, Ex. xxxiv. 28.

[1474] Ex. xxxii. 7; Deut. ix. 12.

[1475] Literally, "in hope of His faith."

[1476] The Greek is here incorrect and unintelligible; and as the Latin omits the clause, our translation is merely conjectural. Hilgenfeld's text, if we give a somewhat peculiar meaning to ellipein, may be translated: "but as it is becoming in one who loves you not to fail in giving you what we have, I, though the very offscouring of you, have been eager to write to you."

[1477] So the Cod. Sin. Hilgenfeld reads, with the Latin, "let us take."

[1478] The Latin here departs entirely from the Greek text, and quotes as a saying of "the Son of God" the following precept, nowhere to be found in the New Testament: "Let us resist all iniquity, and hold it in hatred." Hilgenfeld joins this clause to the former sentence.

[1479] Isa. v. 21.

[1480] An exact quotation from Matt. xx. 16 or Matt. xxii. 14. It is worthy of notice that this is the first example in the writings of the Fathers of a citation from any book of the New Testament, preceded by the authoritative formula, "it is written."

Chapter V.--The new covenant, founded on the sufferings of Christ, tends to our salvation, but to the Jews' destruction.

For to this end the Lord endured to deliver up His flesh to corruption, that we might be sanctified through the remission of sins, which is effected by His blood of sprinkling. For it is written concerning Him, partly with reference to Israel, and partly to us; and [the Scripture] saith thus: "He was wounded for our transgressions, and bruised for our iniquities: with His stripes we are healed. He was brought as a sheep to the slaughter, and as a lamb which is dumb before its shearer." [1481] Therefore we ought to be deeply grateful to the Lord, because He has both made known to us things that are past, and hath given us wisdom concerning things present, and hath not left us without understanding in regard to things which are to come. Now, the Scripture saith, "Not unjustly are nets spread out for birds." [1482] This means that the man perishes justly, who, having a knowledge of the way of righteousness, rushes off into the way of darkness. And further, my brethren: if the Lord endured to suffer for our soul, He being Lord of all the world, to whom God said at the foundation of the world, "Let us make man after our image, and after our likeness," [1483] understand how it was that He endured to suffer at the hand of men. The prophets, having obtained grace from Him, prophesied concerning Him. And He (since it behoved Him to appear in flesh), that He might abolish death, and reveal the resurrection from the dead, endured [what and as He did], in order that He might fulfil the promise made unto the fathers, and by preparing a new people for Himself, might show, while He dwelt on earth, that He, when He has raised mankind, will also judge them. Moreover, teaching Israel, and doing so great miracles and signs, He preached [the truth] to him, and greatly loved him. But when He chose His own apostles who were to preach His Gospel, [He did so from among those] who were sinners above all sin, that He might show He came "not to call the righteous, but sinners to repentance." [1484] Then He manifested Himself to be the Son of God. For if He had not come in the flesh, how could men have been saved by beholding Him? [1485] Since looking upon the sun which is to cease to exist, and is the work of His hands, their eyes are not able to bear his rays. The Son of God therefore came in the flesh with this view, that He might bring to a head the sum of their sins who had persecuted His prophets [1486] to the death. For this purpose, then, He endured. For God saith, "The stroke of his flesh is from them;" [1487] and [1488] "when I shall smite the Shepherd, then the sheep of the flock shall be scattered." [1489] He himself willed thus to suffer, for it was necessary that He should suffer on the tree. For says he who prophesies regarding Him, "Spare my soul from the sword, [1490] fasten my flesh with nails; for the assemblies of the wicked have risen up against me." [1491] And again he says, "Behold, I have given my back to scourges, and my cheeks to strokes, and I have set my countenance as a firm rock." [1492]

[1481] Isa. liii. 5, 7.

[1482] Prov. i. 17, from the LXX, which has mistaken the meaning.

[1483] Gen. i. 26.

[1484] Matt. ix. 13; Mark ii. 17; Luke v. 32.

[1485] The Cod. Sin. reads, "neither would men have been saved by seeing Him."

[1486] Cod. Sin. has, "their prophets," but the corrector has changed it as above.

[1487] A very loose reference to Isa. liii. 8.

[1488] Cod. Sin. omits "and," and reads, "when they smite their own shepherd, then the sheep of the pasture shall be scattered and fail."

[1489] Zech. xiii. 7.

[1490] Cod. Sin. inserts "and."

[1491] These are inaccurate and confused quotations from Ps. xxii. 16, 20, and Ps. cxix. 120.

[1492] Isa. l. 6, 7.

Chapter VI.--The sufferings of Christ, and the new covenant, were announced by the prophets.

When, therefore, He has fulfilled the commandment, what saith He? "Who is he that will contend with Me? let him oppose Me: or who is he that will enter into judgment with Me? let him draw near to the servant of the Lord." [1493] "Woe unto you, for ye shall all wax old, like a garment, and the moth shall eat you up." [1494] And again the prophet says, "Since [1495] as a mighty stone He is laid for crushing, behold I cast down for the foundations of Zion a stone, precious, elect, a corner-stone, honourable." Next, what says He? "And he who shall trust [1496] in it shall live for ever." Is our hope, then, upon a stone? Far from it. But [the language is used] inasmuch as He laid his flesh [as a foundation] with power; for He says, "And He placed me as a firm rock." [1497] And the prophet says again, "The stone which the builders rejected, the same has become the head of the corner." [1498] And again he says, "This is the great and wonderful day which the Lord hath made." [1499] I write the more simply unto you, that ye may understand. I am the off-scouring of your love. [1500] What, then, again says the prophet? "The assembly of the wicked surrounded me; they encompassed me as bees do a honeycomb," [1501] and "upon my garment they cast lots." [1502] Since, therefore, He was about to be manifested and to suffer in the flesh, His suffering was foreshown. For the prophet speaks against Israel, "Woe to their soul, because they have counselled an evil counsel against themselves, [1503] saying, Let us bind the just one, because he is displeasing to us." [1504] And Moses also says to them, [1505] "Behold these things, saith the Lord God: Enter into the good land which the Lord swore [to give] to Abraham, and Isaac, and Jacob, and inherit ye it, a land flowing with milk and honey." [1506] What, then, says Knowledge? [1507] Learn: "Trust," she says, "in Him who is to be manifested to you in the flesh--that is, Jesus." For man is earth in a suffering state, for the formation of Adam was from the face of the earth. What, then, meaneth this: "into the good land, a land flowing with milk and honey?" Blessed be our Lord, who has placed in us wisdom and understanding of secret things. For the prophet says, "Who shall understand the parable of the Lord, except him who is wise and prudent, and who loves his Lord?" [1508] Since, therefore, having renewed us by the remission of our sins, He hath made us after another pattern, [it is His purpose] that we should possess the soul of children, inasmuch as He has created us anew by His Spirit. [1509] For the Scripture says concerning us, while He

speaks to the Son, "Let Us make man after Our image, and
after Our likeness; and let them have dominion over the
beasts of the earth, and the fowls of heaven, and the fishes
of the sea." [1510] And the Lord said, on beholding the fair
creature [1511] man, "Increase, and multiply, and replenish
the earth." [1512] These things [were spoken] to the Son.
Again, I will show thee how, in respect to us, [1513] He has
accomplished a second fashioning in these last days. The
Lord says, "Behold, I will make [1514] the last like the
first." [1515] In reference to this, then, the prophet
proclaimed, "Enter ye into the land flowing with milk and
honey, and have dominion over it." [1516] Behold,
therefore, we have been refashioned, as again He says in
another prophet, "Behold, saith the Lord, I will take away
from these, that is, from those whom the Spirit of the Lord
foresaw, their stony hearts, and I will put hearts of flesh
within them," [1517] because He [1518] was to be
manifested in flesh, and to sojourn among us. For, my
brethren, the habitation of our heart is a holy temple to the
Lord. [1519] For again saith the Lord, "And wherewith shall
I appear before the Lord my God, and be glorified?" [1520]
He says, [1521] "I will confess to thee in the Church in the
midst [1522] of my brethren; and I will praise thee in the
midst of the assembly of the saints." [1523] We, then, are
they whom He has led into the good land. What, then,
mean milk and honey? This, that as the infant is kept alive
first by honey, and then by milk, so also we, being
quickened and kept alive by the faith of the promise and by
the word, shall live ruling over the earth. But He said above,
[1524] "Let them increase, and rule over the fishes." [1525]
Who then is able to govern the beasts, or the fishes, or the
fowls of heaven? For we ought to perceive that to govern

implies authority, so that one should command and rule. If, therefore, this does not exist at present, yet still He has promised it to us. When? When we ourselves also have been made perfect [so as] to become heirs of the covenant of the Lord. [1526]

[1493] Isa. l. 8.

[1494] Isa. l. 9.

[1495] The Latin omits "since," but it is found in all the Greek mss.

[1496] Cod. Sin. has "believe." Isa. viii. 14, Isa. xxviii. 16.

[1497] Isa. l. 7.

[1498] Ps. cxviii. 22.

[1499] Ps. cxviii. 24.

[1500] Comp. 1 Cor. iv. 13. The meaning is, "My love to you is so great, that I am ready to be or to do all things for you."

[1501] Ps. xxii. 17, Ps. cxviii. 12.

[1502] Ps. xxii. 19.

[1503] Isa. iii. 9.

[1504] Wisdom ii. 12. This apocryphal book is thus quoted as Scripture, and intertwined with it.

[1505] Cod. Sin. reads, "What says the other prophet Moses unto them?"

[1506] Ex. xxxiii. 1; Lev. xx. 24.

[1507] The original word is "Gnosis," the knowledge peculiar to advanced Christians, by which they understand the mysteries of Scripture.

[1508] Not found in Scripture. Comp. Isa. xl. 13; Prov. i. 6. Hilgenfeld, however, changes the usual punctuation, which places a colon after prophet, and reads, "For the prophet speaketh the parable of the Lord. Who shall understand," etc.

[1509] The Greek is here very elliptical and obscure: "His Spirit" is inserted above, from the Latin.

[1510] Gen. i. 26.

[1511] Cod. Sin. has "our fair formation."

[1512] Gen. i. 28.

[1513] Cod. Sin. inserts, "the Lord says."

[1514] Cod. Sin. has "I make."

[1515] Not in Scripture, but comp. Matt. xx. 16, and 2 Cor. v. 17.

[1516] Ex. xxxiii. 3.

[1517] Ezek. xi. 19, Ezek. xxxvi. 26.

[1518] Cod. Sin. inserts "Himself;" comp. John i. 14.

[1519] Comp. Eph. ii. 21.

[1520] Comp. Ps. xlii. 2.

[1521] Cod. Sin. omits "He says."

[1522] Cod. Sin. omits "in the midst."

[1523] Ps. xxii. 23; Heb. ii. 12.

[1524] Cod. Sin. has "But we said above."

[1525] Gen. i. 28.

[1526] These are specimens of the "Gnosis," or faculty of bringing out the hidden spiritual meaning of Scripture referred to before. Many more such interpretations follow.

Chapter VII.--Fasting, and the goat sent away, were types of Christ.

Understand, then, ye children of gladness, that the good Lord has foreshown all things to us, that we might know to whom we ought for everything to render thanksgiving and praise. If therefore the Son of God, who is Lord [of all things], and who will judge the living and the dead, suffered, that His stroke might give us life, let us believe that the Son of God could not have suffered except for our sakes. Moreover, when fixed to the cross, He had given Him to drink vinegar and gall. Hearken how the priests of the people [1527] gave previous indications of this. His commandment having been written, the Lord enjoined, that whosoever did not keep the fast should be put to death, because He also Himself was to offer in sacrifice for our sins the vessel of the Spirit, in order that the type established in Isaac when he was offered upon the altar might be fully accomplished. What, then, says He in the prophet? "And let them eat of the goat which is offered, with fasting, for all their sins." [1528] Attend carefully: "And let all the priests alone eat the inwards, unwashed with vinegar." Wherefore? Because to me, who am to offer my flesh for the sins of my new people, ye are to give gall with vinegar to drink: eat ye alone, while the people fast and mourn in sackcloth and ashes. [These things were done] that He might show that it was necessary for Him to suffer for them. [1529] How, [1530] then, ran the commandment? Give your attention. Take two goats of goodly aspect, and similar to each other, and offer them. And let the priest take one as a burnt-offering for sins. [1531] And what should they do with the other? "Accursed," says He, "is the one." Mark how the type of Jesus [1532] now comes out. "And all of you spit upon it, and pierce it, and encircle its head with scarlet wool, and thus let it be driven into the wilderness." And when all this has been done, he who bears the goat brings it into the desert, and takes the wool off from it, and places that upon a shrub which is called Rachia, [1533] of which also we are accustomed to eat the fruits [1534] when we find them in the field. Of this [1535] kind of shrub alone the fruits are sweet. Why then, again, is this? Give good heed. [You see] "one upon the altar, and the other accursed;" and why [do you behold] the one that is accursed crowned? Because they shall see Him then in that day having a scarlet robe about his body down to his feet; and they shall say, Is not this He whom we once despised, and pierced, and mocked, and crucified? Truly this is [1536] He who then declared Himself to be the Son of God. For how like is He to Him! [1537] With a view to this, [He required] the goats to be of goodly aspect, and similar, that, when they see Him then coming, they may be amazed by the likeness of the goat. Behold, then, [1538] the type of Jesus who was to suffer. But why is it that they place the wool in the midst of thorns? It is a type of Jesus set before the view of the Church. [They [1539] place the wool among thorns], that any one who wishes to bear it away may find it necessary to suffer much, because the thorn is formidable, and thus obtain it only as the result of suffering. Thus also, says He, "Those who wish to behold Me, and lay hold of My kingdom, must through tribulation and suffering obtain Me." [1540]

[1527] Cod. Sin. reads "temple," which is adopted by Hilgenfeld.

[1528] Not to be found in Scripture, as is the case also with what follows. Hefele remarks, that "certain false traditions respecting the Jewish rites seem to have prevailed among the Christians of the second century, of which Barnabas here adopts some, as do Justin (Dial. c. Try. 40) and Tertullian (adv. Jud. 14; adv. Marc. iii. 7)."

[1529] Cod. Sin. has "by them."

[1530] Cod. Sin. reads, "what commanded He?"

[1531] Cod. Sin. reads, "one as a burnt-offering, and one for sins."

[1532] Cod. Sin. reads, "type of God," but it has been corrected to "Jesus."

[1533] In Cod. Sin. we find "Rachel." The orthography is doubtful, but there is little question that a kind of bramble-bush is intended.

[1534] Thus the Latin interprets: others render "shoots."

[1535] Cod. Sin. has "thus" instead of "this."

[1536] Literally, "was."

[1537] The text is here in great confusion, though the meaning is plain. Dressel reads, "For how are they alike, and why [does He enjoin] that the goats should be good and alike?" The Cod. Sin. reads, "How is He like Him? For this that," etc.

[1538] Cod. Sin. here inserts "the goat."

[1539] Cod. Sin. reads, "for as he who ... so, says he," etc.

[1540] Comp. Acts xiv. 22.

Chapter VIII.--The red heifer a type of Christ.

Now what do you suppose this to be a type of, that a command was given to Israel, that men of the greatest wickedness [1541] should offer a heifer, and slay and burn it, and, that then boys should take the ashes, and put these into vessels, and bind round a stick [1542] purple wool along with hyssop, and that thus the boys should sprinkle the people, one by one, in order that they might be purified from their sins? Consider how He speaks to you with simplicity. The calf [1543] is Jesus: the sinful men offering it are those who led Him to the slaughter. But now the men are no longer guilty, are no longer regarded as sinners. [1544] And the boys that sprinkle are those that have proclaimed to us the remission of sins and purification of heart. To these He gave authority to preach the Gospel, being twelve in number, corresponding to the twelve tribes [1545] of Israel. But why are there three boys that sprinkle?

To correspond [1546] to Abraham, and Isaac, and Jacob, because these were great with God. And why was the wool [placed] upon the wood? Because by wood Jesus holds His kingdom, so that [through the cross] those believing on Him shall live for ever. But why was hyssop joined with the wool? Because in His kingdom the days will be evil and polluted in which we shall be saved, [and] because he who suffers in body is cured through the cleansing [1547] efficacy of hyssop. And on this account the things which stand thus are clear to us, but obscure to them because they did not hear the voice of the Lord.

[1541] Literally, "men in whom sins are perfect." Of this, and much more that follows, no mention is made in Scripture.

[1542] Cod. Sin. has "upon sticks," and adds, "Behold again the type of the cross, both the scarlet wool and the hyssop,"--adopted by Hilgenfeld.

[1543] Cod. Sin. has, "the law is Christ Jesus," corrected to the above.

[1544] The Greek text is, "then no longer [sinful] men, no longer the glory of sinners," which Dressel defends and Hilgenfeld adopts, but which is surely corrupt.

[1545] Literally, "in witness of the tribes."

[1546] "In witness of."

[1547] Thus the sense seems to require, and thus Dressel translates, though it is difficult to extract such a meaning from the Greek text.

Chapter IX.--The spiritual meaning of circumcision.

He speaks moreover concerning our ears, how He hath circumcised both them and our heart. The Lord saith in the prophet, "In the hearing of the ear they obeyed me." [1548] And again He saith, "By hearing, those shall hear who are afar off; they shall know what I have done." [1549] And, "Be ye circumcised in your hearts, saith the Lord." [1550] And again He says, "Hear, O Israel, for these things saith the Lord thy God." [1551] And once more the Spirit of the Lord proclaims, "Who is he that wishes to live for ever? By hearing let him hear the voice of my servant." [1552] And again He saith, "Hear, O heaven, and give ear, O earth, for God [1553] hath spoken." [1554] These are in proof. [1555] And again He saith, "Hear the word of the Lord, ye rulers of this people." [1556] And again He saith, "Hear, ye children, the voice of one crying in the wilderness." [1557] Therefore He hath circumcised our ears, that we might hear His word and believe, for the circumcision in which they trusted is abolished. [1558] For He declared that circumcision was not of the flesh, but they transgressed because an evil angel deluded them. [1559] He saith to them, "These things saith the Lord your God"--(here [1560] I find a new [1561] commandment)--"Sow not among thorns, but circumcise yourselves to the Lord." [1562] And why speaks He thus: "Circumcise the stubbornness of your heart, and harden not your neck?" [1563] And again: "Behold, saith the Lord, all the nations are uncircumcised [1564] in the flesh, but this people are uncircumcised in heart." [1565] But thou wilt say, "Yea, verily the people are circumcised for a seal." But so also is every Syrian and

Arab, and all the priests of idols: are these then also within the bond of His covenant? [1566] Yea, the Egyptians also practise circumcision. Learn then, my children, concerning all things richly, [1567] that Abraham, the first who enjoined circumcision, looking forward in spirit to Jesus, practised that rite, having received the mysteries [1568] of the three letters. For [the Scripture] saith, "And Abraham circumcised ten, and eight, and three hundred men of his household." [1569] What, then, was the knowledge given to him in this? Learn the eighteen first, and then the three hundred. [1570] The ten and the eight are thus denoted-- Ten by I, and Eight by E. [1571] You have [the initials of the, name of] Jesus. And because [1572] the cross was to express the grace [of our redemption] by the letter T, he says also, "Three Hundred." He signifies, therefore, Jesus by two letters, and the cross by one. He knows this, who has put within us the engrafted [1573] gift of His doctrine. No one has been admitted by me to a more excellent piece of knowledge [1574] than this, but I know that ye are worthy.

[1548] Ps. xviii. 44.

[1549] Isa. xxxiii. 13.

[1550] Jer. iv. 4.

[1551] Jer. vii. 2.

[1552] Ps. xxxiv. 11-13. The first clause of this sentence is wanting in Cod. Sin.

[1553] Cod. Sin. has "Lord."

[1554] Isa. i. 2.

[1555] In proof of the spiritual meaning of circumcision; but Hilgenfeld joins the words to the preceding sentence.

[1556] Isa. i. 10.

[1557] Cod. Sin. reads, "it is the voice," corrected, however, as above.

[1558] Cod. Sin. has, "that we might hear the word, and not only believe," plainly a corrupt text.

[1559] Cod. Sin., at first hand, has "slew them," but is corrected as above.

[1560] The meaning is here very obscure, but the above rendering and punctuation seem preferable to any other.

[1561] Cod. Sin., with several other mss., leaves out "new."

[1562] Jer. iv. 3. Cod. Sin. has "God" instead of "Lord."

[1563] Deut. x. 16.

[1564] This contrast seems to be marked in the original. Cod. Sin. has, "Behold, receive again."

[1565] Jer. ix. 25, 26.

[1566] Dressel and Hilgenfeld read, "their covenant," as does Cod. Sin.; we have followed Hefele.

[1567] Cod. Sin. has "children of love," omitting "richly," and inserting it before "looking forward."

[1568] Literally, "doctrines."

[1569] Not found in Scripture: but comp. Gen. xvii. 26, 27, Gen. xiv. 14.

[1570] Cod. Sin. inserts, "and then making a pause."

[1571] This sentence is altogether omitted by inadvertence in Cod. Sin.

[1572] Some mss. here read, "and further:" the above is the reading in Cod. Sin., and is also that of Hefele.

[1573] This is rendered in the Latin, "the more profound gift," referring, as it does, to the Gnosis of the initiated. The same word is used in chap. i.

[1574] Literally, "has learned a more germane (or genuine) word from me," being an idle vaunt on account of the ingenuity in interpreting Scripture he has just displayed.

Chapter X.--Spiritual significance of the precepts of Moses respecting different kinds of food.

Now, wherefore did Moses say, "Thou shalt not eat the swine, nor the eagle, nor the hawk, nor the raven, nor any fish which is not possessed of scales?" [1575] He embraced three doctrines in his mind [in doing so]. Moreover, the Lord saith to them in Deuteronomy, "And I will establish my ordinances among this people." [1576] Is there then not a command of God [that] they should not eat [these things]? There is, but Moses spoke with a spiritual reference. [1577] For this reason he named the swine, as much as to say, "Thou shalt not join thyself to men who resemble swine." For when they live in pleasure, they forget their Lord; but when they come to want, they acknowledge the Lord. And [in like manner] the swine, when it has eaten, does not recognize its master; but when hungry it cries out, and on receiving food is quiet again. "Neither shalt thou eat," says he "the eagle, nor the hawk, nor the kite, nor the raven." "Thou shalt not join thyself," he means, "to such men as know not how to procure food for themselves by labour and sweat, but seize on that of others in their iniquity, and although wearing an aspect of simplicity, are on the watch to plunder others." [1578] So these birds, while they sit idle, inquire how they may devour the flesh of others, proving themselves pests [to all] by their wickedness. "And thou shalt not eat," he says, "the lamprey, or the polypus, or the cuttlefish." He means, "Thou shalt not join thyself or be like to such men as are ungodly to the end, and are condemned [1579] to death." In like manner as those fishes, above accursed, float in the deep, not swimming [on the surface] like the rest, but make their abode in the mud which lies at the bottom. Moreover, "Thou shall not," he says, "eat the hare." Wherefore? "Thou shall not be a corrupter of boys, nor like unto such." [1580] Because the hare multiplies, year by year, the places of its conception; for as many years as it lives so many [1581] it has. Moreover, "Thou shall not eat the hyena." He means, "Thou shall not be an adulterer, nor a corrupter, nor be like to them that are such." Wherefore? Because that animal annually changes its sex, and is at one time male, and at another female. Moreover, he has rightly detested the weasel. For he means, "Thou shalt not be like to those whom we hear of as committing wickedness with the mouth, [1582] on account of their uncleanness; nor shall thou be joined to those impure women who commit iniquity with the mouth. For this animal conceives by the mouth." Moses then issued [1583] three doctrines concerning meats with a spiritual significance; but they received them according to fleshly desire, as if he had merely spoken of [literal] meats. David, however, comprehends the knowledge of the three doctrines, and speaks in like manner: "Blessed is the man who hath not walked in the counsel of the ungodly," [1584] even as the fishes [referred to] go in darkness to the depths [of the sea]; "and hath not stood in the way of sinners," even as those who profess to fear the Lord, but go astray like swine; "and hath not sat in the seat of scorners," [1585] even as those birds that lie in wait for prey. Take a full and firm grasp of this spiritual [1586] knowledge. But Moses says still further, "Ye shall eat every animal that is cloven-footed and ruminant." What does he mean? [The ruminant animal denotes him] who, on receiving food, recognizes Him that nourishes him, and being satisfied by Him, [1587] is visibly made glad. Well spake [Moses], having respect to the commandment. What, then, does he mean? That we ought to join ourselves to those that fear the Lord, those who meditate in their heart on the commandment which they have received, those who both utter the judgments of the Lord and observe them, those who know that meditation is a work of gladness, and who ruminate [1588] upon the word of the Lord. But what means the cloven-footed? That the righteous man also walks in this world, yet looks forward to the holy state [1589] [to come]. Behold how well Moses legislated. But how was it possible for them to understand or comprehend these things? We then, rightly understanding his commandments, [1590] explain them as the Lord intended. For this purpose He circumcised our ears and our hearts, that we might understand these things.

[1575] Cod. Sin. has "portion," corrected, however, as above. See Lev. xi. and Deut. xiv.

[1576] Deut. iv. 1.

[1577] Literally, "in spirit."

[1578] Cod. Sin. inserts, "and gaze about for some way of escape on account of their greediness, even as these birds alone do not procure food for themselves (by labour), but sitting idle, seek to devour the flesh of others." The text as above seems preferable: Hilgenfeld, however, follows the Greek.

[1579] Cod. Sin. has, "condemned already."

[1580] Dressel has a note upon this passage, in which he refers the words we have rendered, "corrupters of boys," to those who by their dissolute lives waste their fortunes, and so entail destruction on their children; but this does not appear satisfactory. Comp. Clem. Alex. Pædag. ii. 10.

[1581] We have left trupas untranslated. [Cavities, i.e., of conception].

[1582] Cod. Sin. has, "with the body through uncleanness," and so again in the last clause.

[1583] Cod. Sin. inserts, "having received."

[1584] Ps. i. 1.

[1585] Literally, "of the pestilent."

[1586] Cod. Sin. reads, "perfectly," instead of "perfect," as do most mss.; but, according to Dressel, we should read,

"have a perfect knowledge concerning the food."
Hilgenfeld follows the Greek.

[1587] Or, "resting upon Him."

[1588] Cod. Sin. here has the singular, "one who
ruminates."

[1589] Literally, "holy age."

[1590] Cod. Sin. inserts again, "rightly."

Chapter XI.--Baptism and the cross prefigured in the Old Testament.

Let us further inquire whether the Lord took any care to
foreshadow the water [of baptism] and the cross.
Concerning the water, indeed, it is written, in reference to
the Israelites, that they should not receive that baptism
which leads to the remission of sins, but should procure
[1591] another for themselves. The prophet therefore
declares, "Be astonished, O heaven, and let the earth
tremble [1592] at this, because this people hath committed
two great evils: they have forsaken Me, a living fountain,
and have hewn out for themselves broken cisterns. [1593]
Is my holy hill Zion a desolate rock? For ye shall be as the
fledglings of a bird, which fly away when the nest is
removed." [1594] And again saith the prophet, "I will go
before thee and make level the mountains, and will break
the brazen gates, and bruise in pieces the iron bars; and I
will give thee the secret, [1595] hidden, invisible treasures,
that they may know that I am the Lord God." [1596] And
"He shall dwell in a lofty cave of the strong rock." [1597]

Furthermore, what saith He in reference to the Son? "His water is sure; [1598] ye shall see the King in His glory, and your soul shall meditate on the fear of the Lord." [1599] And again He saith in another prophet, "The man who doeth these things shall be like a tree planted by the courses of waters, which shall yield its fruit in due season; and his leaf shall not fade, and all that he doeth shall prosper. Not so are the ungodly, not so, but even as chaff, which the wind sweeps away from the face of the earth. Therefore the ungodly shall not stand in judgment, nor sinners in the counsel of the just; for the Lord knoweth the way of the righteous, but the way of the ungodly shall perish." [1600] Mark how He has described at once both the water and the cross. For these words imply, Blessed are they who, placing their trust in the cross, have gone down into the water; for, says He, they shall receive their reward in due time: then He declares, I will recompense them. But now He saith, [1601] "Their leaves shall not fade." This meaneth, that every word which proceedeth out of your mouth in faith and love shall tend to bring conversion and hope to many. Again, another prophet saith, "And the land of Jacob shall be extolled above every land." [1602] This meaneth the vessel of His Spirit, which He shall glorify. Further, what says He? "And there was a river flowing on the right, and from it arose beautiful trees; and whosoever shall eat of them shall live for ever." [1603] This meaneth, [1604] that we indeed descend into the water full of sins and defilement, but come up, bearing fruit in our heart, having the fear [of God] and trust in Jesus in our spirit. "And whosoever shall eat of these shall live for ever," This meaneth: Whosoever, He declares, shall hear thee speaking, and believe, shall live for ever.

[1591] Literally, "should build."

[1592] Cod. Sin. has, "confine still more," corrected to "tremble still more."

[1593] Cod. Sin. has, "have dug a pit of death." See Jer. ii. 12, 13.

[1594] Comp. Isa. xvi. 1, 2.

[1595] Literally, "dark." Cod. Sin. has, "of darkness."

[1596] Isa. xlv. 2, 3.

[1597] Isa. xxxiii. 16. Cod. Sin. has, "thou shalt dwell."

[1598] Cod. Sin. entirely omits the question given above, and joins "the water is sure" to the former sentence.

[1599] Isa. xxxiii. 16-18.

[1600] Ps. i. 3-6.

[1601] Cod. Sin. has, "what meaneth?"

[1602] Zeph. iii. 19.

[1603] Ezek. xlvii. 12.

[1604] Omitted in Cod. Sin.

Chapter XII.--The cross of Christ frequently announced in the Old Testament.

In like manner He points to the cross of Christ in another prophet, who saith, [1605] "And when shall these things be accomplished? And the Lord saith, When a tree shall be bent down, and again arise, and when blood shall flow out of wood." [1606] Here again you have an intimation concerning the cross, and Him who should be crucified. Yet again He speaks of this [1607] in Moses, when Israel was attacked by strangers. And that He might remind them, when assailed, that it was on account of their sins they were delivered to death, the Spirit speaks to the heart of Moses, that he should make a figure of the cross, [1608] and of Him about to suffer thereon; for unless they put their trust in Him, they shall be overcome for ever. Moses therefore placed one weapon above another in the midst of the hill, [1609] and standing upon it, so as to be higher than all the people, he stretched forth his hands, [1610] and thus again Israel acquired the mastery. But when again he let down his hands, they were again destroyed. For what reason? That they might know that they could not be saved unless they put their trust in Him. [1611] And in another prophet He declares, "All day long I have stretched forth My hands to an unbelieving people, and one that gainsays My righteous way." [1612] And again Moses makes a type of Jesus, [signifying] that it was necessary for Him to suffer, [and also] that He would be the author of life [1613] [to others], whom they believed to have destroyed on the cross [1614] when Israel was falling. For since transgression was committed by Eve through means of the serpent, [the Lord] brought it to pass that every [kind of] serpents bit them, and they died, [1615] that He might convince them, that on account of their transgression they were given over to the straits of death. Moreover Moses, when he commanded, "Ye shall not have any graven or molten [image] for your God," [1616] did so that he might reveal a type of Jesus. Moses then makes a brazen serpent, and places it upon a beam, [1617] and by proclamation assembles the people. When, therefore, they were come together, they besought Moses that he would offer sacrifice [1618] in their behalf, and pray for their recovery. And Moses spake unto them, saying, "When any one of you is bitten, let him come to the serpent placed on the pole; and let him hope and believe, that even though dead, it is able to give him life, and immediately he shall be restored." [1619] And they did so. Thou hast in this also [an indication of] the glory of Jesus; for in Him and to Him are all things. [1620] What, again, says Moses to Jesus (Joshua) the son of Nave, when he gave him [1621] this name, as being a prophet, with this view only, that all the people might hear that the Father would reveal all things concerning His Son Jesus to the son [1622] of Nave? This name then being given him when he sent him to spy out the land, he said, "Take a book into thy hands, and write what the Lord declares, that the Son of God will in the last days cut off from the roots all the house of Amalek." [1623] Behold again: Jesus who was manifested, both by type and in the flesh, [1624] is not the Son of man, but the Son of God. Since, therefore, they were to say that Christ was the son [1625] of David, fearing and understanding the error of the wicked, he saith, "The Lord said unto my Lord, Sit at My right hand, until I make Thine enemies Thy footstool." [1626] And again, thus saith Isaiah, "The Lord said to Christ, [1627] my Lord, whose right hand I have holden, [1628] that the nations should yield obedience before Him; and I will break in pieces the strength of kings." [1629] Behold how David calleth Him Lord and the Son of God.

[1605] Cod. Sin. refers this to God, and not to the prophet.

[1606] From some unknown apocryphal book. Hilgenfeld compares Hab. ii. 11.

[1607] Cod. Sin. reads, "He speaks to Moses."

[1608] Cod. Sin. omits "and."

[1609] Cod. Sin. reads pugmes, which must here be translated "heap" or "mass." According to Hilgenfeld, however, pugme is here equivalent to pugmachia, "a fight." The meaning would then be, that "Moses piled weapon upon weapon in the midst of the battle," instead of "hill" (peges), as above.

[1610] Thus standing in the form of a cross.

[1611] Or, as some read, "in the cross."

[1612] Isa. lxv. 2.

[1613] Cod. Sin. has, "and He shall make him alive."

[1614] Literally, "the sign."

[1615] Comp. Num. xxi. 6-9; John iii. 14-18.

[1616] Deut. xxvii. 15. Cod. Sin. reads, "molten or graven."

[1617] Instead of en doko, "on a beam," Cod. Sin. with other mss. has endoxos, "manifestly," which is adopted by Hilgenfeld.

[1618] Cod. Sin. simply reads, "offer supplication."

[1619] Num. xxi. 9.

[1620] Comp. Col. i. 16.

[1621] Cod. Sin. has the imperative, "Put on him;" but it is connected as above.

[1622] Cod. Sin. closes the sentence with Jesus, and inserts, "Moses said therefore to Jesus."

[1623] Ex. xvii. 14.

[1624] Comp. 1 Tim. iii. 16.

[1625] That is, merely human: a reference is supposed to the Ebionites.

[1626] Ps. cx. 1; Matt. xxii. 43-45.

[1627] Cod. Sin. corrects "to Cyrus," as LXX.

[1628] Cod. Sin. has, "he has taken hold."

[1629] Isa. xlv. 1.

Chapter XIII.--Christians, and not Jews, the heirs of the covenant.

But let us see if this people [1630] is the heir, or the former, and if the covenant belongs to us or to them. Hear ye now what the Scripture saith concerning the people. Isaac prayed for Rebecca his wife, because she was barren; and she conceived. [1631] Furthermore also, Rebecca went forth to inquire of the Lord; and the Lord said to her, "Two nations are in thy womb, and two peoples in thy belly; and the one people shall surpass the other, and the elder shall serve the younger." [1632] You ought to understand who was Isaac, who Rebecca, and concerning what persons He declared that this people should be greater than that. And in another prophecy Jacob speaks more clearly to his son Joseph, saying, "Behold, the Lord hath not deprived me of thy presence; bring thy sons to me, that I may bless them." [1633] And he brought Manasseh and Ephraim, desiring that Manasseh [1634] should be blessed, because he was the elder. With this view Joseph led him to the right hand of his father Jacob. But Jacob saw in spirit the type of the people to arise afterwards. And what says [the Scripture]? And Jacob changed the direction of his hands, and laid his right hand upon the head of Ephraim, the second and younger, and blessed him. And Joseph said to Jacob, "Transfer thy right hand to the head of Manasseh, [1635] for he is my first-born son." [1636] And Jacob said, "I know it, my son, I know it; but the elder shall serve the younger: yet he also shall be blessed." [1637] Ye see on whom he laid [1638] [his hands], that this people should be first, and heir of the covenant. If then, still further, the same thing was intimated through Abraham, we reach the perfection of our knowledge. What, then, says He to Abraham? "Because thou hast believed, [1639] it is imputed to thee for righteousness: behold, I have made thee the father of those nations who believe in the Lord while in [a state of] uncircumcision." [1640]

[1630] That is, "Christians."

[1631] Gen. xxv. 21.

[1632] Gen. xxv. 23.

[1633] Gen. xlviii. 11, 9.

[1634] Cod. Sin. reads each time "Ephraim," by a manifest mistake, instead of Manasseh.

[1635] Cod. Sin. reads each time "Ephraim," by a manifest mistake, instead of Manasseh.

[1636] Gen. xlviii. 18.

[1637] Gen. xlviii. 19.

[1638] Or, "of whom he willed."

[1639] Cod. Sin. has, "when alone believing," and is followed by Hilgenfeld to this effect: "What, then, says He to Abraham, when, alone believing, he was placed in righteousness? Behold," etc.

[1640] Gen. xv. 6, Gen. xvii. 5; comp. Rom. iv. 3.

Chapter XIV.--The Lord hath given us the testament which Moses received and broke.

Yes [it is even so]; but let us inquire if the Lord has really given that testament which He swore to the fathers that He would give [1641] to the people. He did give it; but they were not worthy to receive it, on account of their sins. For the prophet declares, "And Moses was fasting forty days and forty nights on Mount Sinai, that he might receive the testament of the Lord for the people." [1642] And he received from the Lord [1643] two tables, written in the spirit by the finger of the hand of the Lord. And Moses having received them, carried them down to give to the people. And the Lord said to Moses, "Moses, Moses, go down quickly; for thy people hath sinned, whom thou didst bring out of the land of Egypt." [1644] And Moses understood that they had again [1645] made molten images; and he threw the tables out of his hands, and the tables of the testament of the Lord were broken. Moses then received it, but they proved themselves unworthy. Learn now how we have received it. Moses, as a servant, [1646] received it; but the Lord himself, having suffered in our behalf, hath given it to us, that we should be the people of inheritance. But He was manifested, in order that they might be perfected in their iniquities, and that we, being constituted heirs through Him, [1647] might receive the testament of the Lord Jesus, who was prepared for this end, that by His personal manifestation, redeeming our hearts (which were already wasted by death, and given over to the iniquity of error) from darkness, He might by His word enter into a covenant with us. For it is written how the Father, about to redeem [1648] us from darkness, commanded Him to prepare [1649] a holy people for Himself. The prophet therefore declares, "I, the Lord Thy God, have called Thee in righteousness, and will hold Thy hand, and will strengthen Thee; and I have given Thee for a covenant to the people, for a light to the nations, to open the eyes of the blind, and to bring forth from fetters them that are bound, and those that sit in darkness out of the prison-house." [1650] Ye perceive, [1651] then, whence we have been redeemed. And again, the prophet says, "Behold, I have appointed Thee as a light to the nations, that Thou mightest be for salvation even to the ends of the earth, saith the Lord God that redeemeth thee." [1652] And again, the prophet saith, "The Spirit of the Lord is upon me; because He hath anointed me to preach the Gospel to the humble: He hath sent me to heal the broken-hearted, to proclaim deliverance to the captives, and recovery of sight to the blind; to announce the acceptable year of the Lord, and the day of recompense; to comfort all that mourn." [1653]

[1641] Cod. Sin. absurdly repeats "to give."

[1642] Ex. xxiv. 18.

[1643] Ex. xxxi. 18.

[1644] Ex. xxxii. 7; Deut. ix. 12.

[1645] Cod. Sin. reads, "for themselves."

[1646] Comp. Heb. iii. 5.

[1647] Cod. Sin. and other mss. read, "through Him who inherited."

[1648] Cod. Sin. refers this to Christ.

[1649] Cod. Sin. reads, "be prepared." Hilgenfeld follows Cod. Sin. so far, and reads, "For it is written how the Father commanded Him who was to redeem us from darkness (auto--lutrosamenos) to prepare a holy people for Himself."

[1650] Isa. xlii. 6, 7.

[1651] Cod. Sin. has, "we know."

[1652] Isa. xlix. 6. The text of Cod. Sin., and of the other mss., is here in great confusion: we have followed that given by Hefele.

[1653] Isa. lxi. 1, 2.

Chapter XV.--The false and the true Sabbath.

Further, [1654] also, it is written concerning the Sabbath in the Decalogue which [the Lord] spoke, face to face, to Moses on Mount Sinai, "And sanctify ye the Sabbath of the Lord with clean hands and a pure heart." [1655] And He says in another place, "If my sons keep the Sabbath, then will I cause my mercy to rest upon them." [1656] The Sabbath is mentioned at the beginning of the creation [thus]: "And God made in six days the works of His hands, and made an end on the seventh day, and rested on it, and sanctified it." [1657] Attend, my children, to the meaning of this expression, "He finished in six days." This implieth that the Lord will finish all things in six thousand years, for a day is [1658] with Him a thousand years. And He Himself testifieth, [1659] saying, "Behold, to-day [1660] will be as a thousand years." [1661] Therefore, my children, in six days, that is, in six thousand years, all things will be finished. "And He rested on the seventh day." This meaneth: when His Son, coming [again], shall destroy the time of the wicked man, [1662] and judge the ungodly, and change the sun, and the moon, [1663] and the stars, then shall He truly rest on the seventh day. Moreover, He says, "Thou shalt sanctify it with pure hands and a pure heart." If, therefore, any one can now sanctify the day which God hath sanctified, except he is pure in heart in all things, [1664] we are deceived. [1665] Behold, therefore: [1666] certainly then one properly resting sanctifies it, when we ourselves, having received the promise, wickedness no longer existing, and all things having been made new by the Lord, shall be able to work righteousness. [1667] Then we shall be able to sanctify it, having been first sanctified ourselves. [1668] Further, He says to them, "Your new moons and your Sabbaths I cannot endure." [1669] Ye perceive how He speaks: Your present Sabbaths are not acceptable to Me, but that is which I have made, [namely this,] when, giving rest to all things, I shall make a beginning of the eighth day, that is, a beginning of another world. Wherefore, also, we keep the eighth day with joyfulness, the day also on which Jesus rose again from the dead. [1670] And [1671] when He had manifested Himself, He ascended into the heavens.

[1654] Cod. Sin. reads "because," but this is corrected to "moreover."

[1655] Ex. xx. 8; Deut. v. 12.

[1656] Jer. xvii. 24, 25.

[1657] Gen. ii. 2. The Hebrew text is here followed, the Septuagint reading "sixth" instead of "seventh."

[1658] Cod. Sin. reads "signifies."

[1659] Cod. Sin. adds, "to me."

[1660] Cod. Sin. reads, "The day of the Lord shall be as a thousand years."

[1661] Ps. xc. 4; 2 Pet. iii. 8.

[1662] Cod. Sin. seems properly to omit "of the wicked man."

[1663] Cod. Sin. places stars before moon.

[1664] Cod. Sin. reads "again," but is corrected as above.

[1665] The meaning is, "If the Sabbaths of the Jews were the true Sabbath, we should have been deceived by God, who demands pure hands and a pure heart."--Hefele.

[1666] Cod. Sin. has, "But if not." Hilgenfeld's text of this confused passage reads as follows: "Who then can sanctify the day which God has sanctified, except the man who is of a pure heart? We are deceived (or mistaken) in all things. Behold, therefore," etc.

[1667] Cod. Sin. reads, "resting aright, we shall sanctify it, having been justified, and received the promise, iniquity no longer existing, but all things having been made new by the Lord."

[1668] Cod. Sin. reads, "Shall we not then?"

[1669] Isa. i. 13.

[1670] "Barnabas here bears testimony to the observance of the Lord's Day in early times."--Hefele.

[1671] We here follow the punctuation of Dressel: Hefele places only a comma between the clauses, and inclines to think that the writer implies that the ascension of Christ took place on the first day of the week.

Chapter XVI.--The spiritual temple of God.

Moreover, I will also tell you concerning the temple, how the wretched [Jews], wandering in error, trusted not in God Himself, but in the temple, as being the house of God. For almost after the manner of the Gentiles they worshipped Him in the temple. [1672] But learn how the Lord speaks, when abolishing it: "Who hath meted out heaven with a span, and the earth with his palm? Have not I?" [1673] "Thus saith the Lord, Heaven is My throne, and the earth My footstool: what kind of house will ye build to Me, or what is the place of My rest?" [1674] Ye perceive that their hope is vain. Moreover, He again says, "Behold, they who have cast down this temple, even they shall build it up again." [1675] It has so happened. [1676] For through their going to war, it was destroyed by their enemies; and now they, as the servants of their enemies, shall rebuild it. Again, it was revealed that the city and the temple and the people of Israel were to be given up. For the Scripture saith, "And it shall come to pass in the last days, that the Lord will deliver up the sheep of His pasture, and their sheep-fold and tower, to destruction." [1677] And it so happened as the Lord had spoken. Let us inquire, then, if there still is a temple of God. There is--where He himself declared He would make and finish it. For it is written, "And it shall come to pass, when the week is completed, the temple of God shall be built in glory in the name of the Lord." [1678] I find, therefore, that a temple does exist. Learn, then, how it shall be built in the name of the Lord. Before we believed in God, the habitation of our heart was corrupt and weak, as being indeed like a temple made with hands. For it was full of idolatry, and was a habitation of demons, through our doing such things as were opposed to [the will of] God. But it shall be built, observe ye, in the name of the Lord, in order that the temple of the Lord may be built in glory. How? Learn [as follows]. Having received the forgiveness of sins, and placed our trust in the name of the Lord, we have become new creatures, formed again from the beginning. Wherefore in our habitation God truly dwells in us. How? His word of faith; His calling [1679] of promise; the wisdom of the statutes; the commands of the doctrine; He himself prophesying in us; He himself dwelling in us; opening to us who were enslaved by death the doors of the temple, that is, the mouth; and by giving us repentance introduced us into the incorruptible temple. [1680] He then, who wishes to be saved, looks not to man, [1681] but to Him who dwelleth in him, and speaketh in him, amazed at never having either heard him utter such words with his mouth, nor himself having ever desired to hear them. [1682] This is the spiritual temple built for the Lord.

[1672] That is, "they worshipped the temple instead of Him."

[1673] Isa. xl. 12.

[1674] Isa. lxvi. 1.

[1675] Comp. Isa. xlix. 17 (Sept.).

[1676] Cod. Sin. omits this.

[1677] Comp. Isa. v., Jer. xxv.; but the words do not occur in Scripture.

[1678] Dan. ix. 24-27; Hag. ii. 10.

[1679] Cod. Sin. reads, "the calling."

[1680] Cod. Sin. gives the clauses of this sentence separately, each occupying a line.

[1681] That is, the man who is engaged in preaching the Gospel.

[1682] Such is the punctuation adopted by Hefele, Dressel, and Hilgenfeld.

Chapter XVII.--Conclusion of the first part of the epistle.

As far as was possible, and could be done with perspicuity, I cherish the hope that, according to my desire, I have omitted none [1683] of those things at present [demanding consideration], which bear upon your salvation. For if I should write to you about things future, [1684] ye would not understand, because such knowledge is hid in parables. These things then are so.

 [1683] Cod. Sin. reads, "my soul hopes that it has not omitted anything."

[1684] Cod. Sin., "about things present or future." Hilgenfeld's text of this passage is as follows: "My mind and soul hopes that, according to my desire, I have omitted none of the things that pertain to salvation. For if I should write to you about things present or future," etc. Hefele gives the text as above, and understands the meaning to be, "points bearing on the present argument."

Chapter XVIII.--Second part of the epistle. The two ways.

But let us now pass to another sort of knowledge and doctrine. There are two ways of doctrine and authority, the one of light, and the other of darkness. But there is a great difference between these two ways. For over one are stationed the light-bringing angels of God, but over the other the angels [1685] of Satan. And He indeed (i.e., God) is Lord for ever and ever, but he (i.e., Satan) is prince of the time [1686] of iniquity.

[1685] Comp. 2 Cor. xii. 7.

[1686] Cod. Sin. reads, "of the present time of iniquity."

Chapter XIX.--The way of light.

The way of light, then, is as follows. If any one desires to travel to the appointed place, he must be zealous in his works. The knowledge, therefore, which is given to us for the purpose of walking in this way, is the following. Thou shalt love Him that created thee: [1687] thou shalt glorify Him that redeemed thee from death. Thou shalt be simple in heart, and rich in spirit. Thou shalt not join thyself to those who walk in the way of death. Thou shalt hate doing what is unpleasing to God: thou shalt hate all hypocrisy. Thou shalt not forsake the commandments of the Lord. Thou shalt not exalt thyself, but shalt be of a lowly mind. [1688] Thou shalt not take glory to thyself. Thou shalt not take evil counsel against thy neighbour. Thou shalt not allow over-boldness to enter into thy soul. [1689] Thou shalt not commit fornication: thou shalt not commit adultery: thou shalt not be a corrupter of youth. Thou shalt not let the word of God issue from thy lips with any kind of impurity. [1690] Thou shalt not accept persons when thou reprovest any one for transgression. Thou shalt be meek: thou shalt be peaceable. Thou shalt tremble at the words which thou hearest. [1691] Thou shalt not be mindful of evil against thy brother. Thou shalt not be of doubtful mind [1692] as to whether a thing shall be or not. Thou shalt not take the name [1693] of the Lord in vain. Thou shalt love thy neighbour more than thine own soul. [1694] Thou shalt not slay the child by procuring abortion; nor, again, shalt thou destroy it after it is born. Thou shalt not withdraw thy hand from thy son, or from thy daughter, but from their infancy thou shalt teach them the fear of the Lord. [1695] Thou shalt not covet what is thy neighbour's, nor shalt thou be avaricious. Thou shalt not be joined in soul with the haughty, but thou shalt be reckoned with the righteous and lowly. Receive thou as good things the trials [1696] which come upon thee. [1697] Thou shalt not be of double mind or of double tongue, [1698] for a double tongue is a snare of death. Thou shalt be subject [1699] to the Lord, and to [other] masters as the image of God, with modesty and fear. Thou shalt not issue orders with bitterness to thy maidservant or thy man-servant, who trust in the same [God [1700]], lest thou shouldst not [1701] reverence that God who is above both; for He came to call men not according to their outward appearance, [1702] but according as the Spirit had prepared them. [1703] Thou shalt communicate in all things with thy neighbour; thou shalt not call [1704] things thine own; for if ye are partakers in common of things which are incorruptible, [1705] how much more [should you be] of those things which are corruptible! [1706] Thou shalt not be hasty with thy tongue, for the mouth is a snare of death. As far as possible, thou shalt be pure in thy soul. Do not be ready to stretch forth thy hands to take, whilst thou contractest them to give. Thou shalt love, as the apple of thine eye, every one that speaketh to thee the word of the Lord. Thou shalt remember the day of judgment, night and day. Thou shalt seek out every day the faces of the saints, [1707] either by word examining them, and going to exhort them, and meditating how to save a soul by the word, [1708] or by thy hands thou shalt labour for the redemption of thy sins. Thou shalt not hesitate to give, nor murmur when thou givest. "Give to every one that asketh thee," [1709] and thou shalt know who is the good Recompenser of the reward. Thou shalt preserve what thou hast received [in charge], neither adding to it nor taking from it. To the last thou shalt hate the wicked [1710] [one]. [1711] Thou shalt judge righteously. Thou shalt not make a schism, but thou shalt pacify those that contend by bringing them together. Thou shalt confess thy sins. Thou shalt not go to prayer with an evil conscience. This is the way of light. [1712]

[1687] Cod. Sin. inserts, "Thou shalt fear Him that formed thee."

[1688] Cod. Sin. adds, "in all things."

[1689] Literally, "shalt not give insolence to thy soul."

[1690] "That is, while proclaiming the Gospel, thou shalt not in any way be of corrupt morals."--Hefele.

[1691] Isa. lxvi. 2. All the preceding clauses are given in Cod. Sin. in distinct lines.

[1692] Comp. Jas. i. 8.

[1693] Cod. Sin. has "thy name," but this is corrected as above.

[1694] Cod. Sin. corrects to, "as thine own soul."

[1695] Cod. Sin. has, "of God."

[1696] "Difficulties," or "troubles."

[1697] Cod. Sin. adds, "knowing that without God nothing happens."

[1698] Cod. Sin. has, "talkative," and omits the following clause.

[1699] Cod. Sin. has, "Thou shalt be subject (hupotagese-- untouched by the corrector) to masters as a type of God."

[1700] Inserted in Cod. Sin.

[1701] Cod. Sin. has, "they should not."

[1702] Comp. Eph. vi. 9.

[1703] Comp. Rom. viii. 29, 30.

[1704] Cod. Sin. has, "and not call."

[1705] Cod. Sin. has, "in that which is incorruptible."

[1706] Cod. Sin. has, "in things that are subject to death," but is corrected as above.

[1707] Or, "the persons of the saints." Cod. Sin. omits this clause, but it is added by the corrector.

[1708] The text is here confused in all the editions; we have followed that of Dressel. Cod. Sin. is defective. Hilgenfeld's text reads, "Thou shalt seek out every day the faces of the saints, either labouring by word and going to exhort them, and meditating to save a soul by the word, or by thy hands thou shalt labour for the redemption of thy sins"--almost identical with that given above.

[1709] Cod. Sin. omits this quotation from Matt. v. 42 or Luke vi. 30, but it is added by a corrector.

[1710] Cod. Sin. has, "hate evil."

[1711] Cod. Sin. inserts "and."

[1712] Cod. Sin. omits this clause: it is inserted by a corrector.

Chapter XX.--The way of darkness.

But the way of darkness [1713] is crooked, and full of cursing; for it is the way of eternal [1714] death with punishment, in which way are the things that destroy the soul, viz., idolatry, over-confidence, the arrogance of power, hypocrisy, double-heartedness, adultery, murder, rapine, haughtiness, transgression, [1715] deceit, malice, self-sufficiency, poisoning, magic, avarice, [1716] want of the fear of God. [In this way, too,] are those who persecute the good, those who hate truth, those who love falsehood, those who know not the reward of righteousness, those who cleave not to that which is good, those who attend not with just judgment to the widow and orphan, those who watch not to the fear of God, [but incline] to wickedness, from whom meekness and patience are far off; persons who love vanity, follow after a reward, pity not the needy, labour not in aid of him who is overcome with toil; who are prone to evil-speaking, who know not Him that made them, who are murderers of children, destroyers of the workmanship of God; who turn away him that is in want, who oppress the afflicted, who are advocates of the rich, who are unjust judges of the poor, and who are in every respect transgressors.

[1713] Literally, "of the Black One."

[1714] Cod. Sin. joins "eternal" with way, instead of death.

[1715] Cod. Sin. reads "transgressions."

[1716] Cod. Sin. omits "magic, avarice."

Chapter XXI.--Conclusion.

It is well, therefore, [1717] that he who has learned the judgments of the Lord, as many as have been written, should walk in them. For he who keepeth these shall be glorified in the kingdom of God; but he who chooseth other things [1718] shall be destroyed with his works. On this account there will be a resurrection, [1719] on this account a retribution. I beseech you who are superiors, if you will receive any counsel of my good-will, have among yourselves those to whom you may show kindness: do not forsake them. For the day is at hand on which all things shall perish with the evil [one]. The Lord is near, and His reward. Again, and yet again, I beseech you: be good lawgivers [1720] to one another; continue faithful counsellors of one another; take away from among you all hypocrisy. And may God, who ruleth over all the world, give to you wisdom, intelligence, understanding, knowledge of His judgments, [1721] with patience. And be ye [1722] taught of God, inquiring diligently what the Lord asks from

you; and do it that ye maybe safe in the day of judgment.
[1723] And if you have any remembrance of what is good,
be mindful of me, meditating on these things, in order that
both my desire and watchfulness may result in some good. I
beseech you, entreating this as a favour. While yet you are
in this fair vessel, [1724] do not fail in any one of those
things, [1725] but unceasingly seek after them, and fulfil
every commandment; for these things are worthy. [1726]
Wherefore I have been the more earnest to write to you, as
my ability served, [1727] that I might cheer you. Farewell,
ye children of love and peace. The Lord of glory and of all
grace be with your spirit. Amen. [1728]

[1717] Cod. Sin. omits "therefore."

[1718] The things condemned in the previous chapter.

[1719] Cod. Sin. has "resurrections," but is corrected as
above.

[1720] Cod. Sin. has, "lawgivers of good things."

[1721] Cod. Sin. omits the preposition.

[1722] Cod. Sin. omits this.

[1723] Cod. Sin. reads, "that ye may be found in the day of
judgment," which Hilgenfeld adopts.

[1724] Literally, "While yet the good vessel is with you," i.e.,
as long as you are in the body.

[1725] Cod. Sin. reads, "fail not in any one of yourselves,"
which is adopted by Hilgenfeld.

[1726] Corrected in Cod. Sin. to, "it is worthy."

[1727] Cod. Sin. omits this clause, but it is inserted by the corrector.

[1728] Cod. Sin. omits "Amen," and adds at the close, "Epistle of Barnabas."

[1444] The Codex Sinaiticus has simply "Epistle of Barnabas" for title; Dressel gives, "Epistle of Barnabas the Apostle," from the Vatican ms. of the Latin text.

Papias

Introductory Note to the Fragments of Papias

[a.d. 70-155.] It seems unjust to the holy man of whose comparatively large contributions to early Christian literature such mere relics have been preserved, to set them forth in these versions, unaccompanied by the copious annotations of Dr. Routh. If even such crumbs from his table are not by any means without a practical value, with reference to the Canon and other matters, we may well credit the testimony (though disputed) of Eusebius, that he was a learned man, and well versed in the Holy Scripture. [1729] All who name poor Papias are sure to do so with the apologetic qualification of that historian, that he was of slender capacity. Nobody who attributes to him the millenarian fancies, of which he was but a narrator, as if these were the characteristics rather than the blemishes of his works, can fail to accept this estimate of our author. But more may be said when we come to the great name of Irenæus, who seems to make himself responsible for them. [1730]

Papias has the credit of association with Polycarp, in the friendship of St. John himself, and of "others who had seen the Lord." He is said to have been bishop of Hierapolis, in Phrygia, and to have died about the same time that Polycarp suffered; but even this is questioned. So little do we know of one whose lost books, could they be recovered, might reverse the received judgment, and establish his claim to the disputed tribute which makes him, like Apollos, "an eloquent man, and mighty in the Scriptures."

The following is the original Introductory Notice:--

The principal information in regard to Papias is given in the extracts made among the fragments from the works of Irenæus and Eusebius. He was bishop of the Church in Hierapolis, a city of Phrygia, in the first half of the second century. Later writers affirm that he suffered martyrdom about a.d. 163; some saying that Rome, others that Pergamus, was the scene of his death. He was a hearer of the Apostle John, and was on terms of intimate intercourse with many who had known the Lord and His apostles. From these he gathered the floating traditions in regard to the sayings of our Lord, and wove them into a production divided into five books. This work does not seem to have been confined to an exposition of the sayings of Christ, but to have contained much historical information.

Eusebius [1731] speaks of Papias as a man most learned in all things, and well acquainted with the Scriptures. In another passage [1732] he describes him as of small capacity. The fragments of Papias are translated from the text given in Routh's Reliquiæ Sacræ, vol. i. [1733]

[1729] See Lardner, ii. p. 119.

[1730] Against Heresies, book v. chap. xxxiii. See the prudent note of Canon Robertson (History of the Christ. Church, vol. i. p. 116).

[1731] Hist. Eccl., iii. 39.

[1732] Ibid.

[1733] [Where the fragments with learned annotations and elucidations fill forty-four pages.]

Fragments of Papias

I. From the exposition of the oracles of the Lord. [1734]

[The writings of Papias in common circulation are five in number, and these are called an Exposition of the Oracles of the Lord. Irenæus makes mention of these as the only works written by him, in the following words: "Now testimony is borne to these things in writing by Papias, an ancient man, who was a hearer of John, and a friend of Polycarp, in the fourth of his books; for five books were composed by him." Thus wrote Irenæus. Moreover, Papias himself, in the introduction to his books, makes it manifest that he was not himself a hearer and eye-witness of the holy apostles; but he tells us that he received the truths of our religion [1735] from those who were acquainted with them [the apostles] in the following words:]

But I shall not be unwilling to put down, along with my interpretations, [1736] whatsoever instructions I received with care at any time from the elders, and stored up with care in my memory, assuring you at the same time of their truth. For I did not, like the multitude, take pleasure in those who spoke much, but in those who taught the truth; nor in those who related strange commandments, [1737] but in those who rehearsed the commandments given by the Lord to faith, [1738] and proceeding from truth itself. If, then, any one who had attended on the elders came, I asked minutely after their sayings,--what Andrew or Peter said, or what was said by Philip, or by Thomas, or by James, or by John, or by Matthew, or by any other of the Lord's disciples: which things [1739] Aristion and the presbyter John, the disciples of the Lord, say. For I imagined that what was to be got from books was not so profitable to me as what came from the living and abiding voice.

[1734] This fragment is found in Eusebius, Hist. Eccl. iii. 39.

[1735] Literally, "the things of faith."

[1736] Papias states that he will give an exact account of what the elders said; and that, in addition to this, he will accompany this account with an explanation of the meaning and import of the statements.

[1737] Literally, "commandments belonging to others," and therefore strange and novel to the followers of Christ.

[1738] Given to faith has been variously understood. Either not stated in direct language, but like parables given in figures, so that only the faithful could understand; or entrusted to faith, that is, to those who were possessed of faith, the faithful.

[1739] Which things: this is usually translated, "what Aristion and John say;" and the translation is admissible. But the words more naturally mean, that John and Aristion, even at the time of his writing, were telling him some of the sayings of the Lord.

II. [1740]

[The early Christians] called those who practised a godly guilelessness, [1741] children, [as is stated by Papias in the first book of the Lord's Expositions, and by Clemens Alexandrinus in his Pædagogue.]

[1740] This fragment is found in the Scholia of Maximus on the works of Dionysius the Areopagite.

[1741] Literally, "a guilelessness according to God."

III. [1742]

Judas walked about in this world a sad [1743] example of impiety; for his body having swollen to such an extent that he could not pass where a chariot could pass easily, he was crushed by the chariot, so that his bowels gushed out. [1744]

[1742] This fragment is found in OEcumenius.

[1743] Literally, "great."

[1744] Literally, "were emptied out." Theophylact, after quoting this passage, adds other particulars, as if they were derived from Papias. [But see Routh, i. pp. 26, 27.] He says that Judas's eyes were so swollen that they could not be seen, even by the optical instruments of physicians; and that the rest of his body was covered with runnings and worms. He further states, that he died in a solitary spot, which was left desolate until his time; and no one could pass the place without stopping up his nose with his hands.

IV. [1745]

As the elders who saw John the disciple of the Lord remembered that they had heard from him how the Lord taught in regard to those times, and said]: "The days will come in which vines shall grow, having each ten thousand branches, and in each branch ten thousand twigs, and in each true twig ten thousand shoots, and in every one of the shoots ten thousand clusters, and on every one of the clusters ten thousand grapes, and every grape when pressed will give five-and-twenty metretes of wine. And when any one of the saints shall lay hold of a cluster, another shall cry out, I am a better cluster, take me; bless the Lord through me.' In like manner, [He said] that a grain of wheat would produce ten thousand ears, and that every ear would have ten thousand grains, and every grain would yield ten pounds of clear, pure, fine flour; and that apples, and seeds, and grass would produce in similar proportions; and that all animals, feeding then only on the productions of the earth, would become peaceable and harmonious, and be in perfect subjection to man." [1746] [Testimony is borne to these things in writing by Papias, an ancient man, who was a hearer of John and a friend of Polycarp, in the fourth of his books; for five books were composed by him. And he added, saying, "Now these things are credible to believers. And Judas the traitor," says he, "not believing, and asking, How shall such growths be accomplished by the Lord?' the Lord said, They shall see who shall come to them.' These, then, are the times mentioned by the prophet Isaiah: And the wolf shall lie down with the lamb,' etc. (Isa. xi. 6 ff.)."]

[1745] From Irenæus, Hær., v. 32. [Hearsay at second-hand, and handed about among many, amounts to nothing as evidence. Note the reports of sermons, also, as they appear in our daily Journals. Whose reputation can survive if such be credited?]

[1746] [See Grabe, apud Routh, 1. 29.]

V. [1747]

As the presbyters say, then [1748] those who are deemed
worthy of an abode in heaven shall go there, others shall
enjoy the delights of Paradise, and others shall possess the
splendour of the city; [1749] for everywhere the Saviour will
be seen, according as they shall be worthy who see Him.
But that there is this distinction between the habitation of
those who produce an hundred-fold, and that of those who
produce sixty-fold, and that of those who produce thirty-
fold; for the first will be taken up into the heavens, the
second class will dwell in Paradise, and the last will inhabit
the city; and that on this account the Lord said, "In my
Father's house are many mansions:" [1750] for all things
belong to God, who supplies all with a suitable dwelling-
place, even as His word says, that a share is given to all by
the Father, [1751] according as each one is or shall be
worthy. And this is the couch [1752] in which they shall
recline who feast, being invited to the wedding. The
presbyters, the disciples of the apostles, say that this is the
gradation and arrangement of those who are saved, and that
they advance through steps of this nature; and that,
moreover, they ascend through the Spirit to the Son, and
through the Son to the Father; and that in due time the Son
will yield up His work to the Father, even as it is said by the
apostle, "For He must reign till He hath put all enemies
under His feet. The last enemy that shall be destroyed is
death." [1753] For in the times of the kingdom the just man
who is on the earth shall forget to die. "But when He saith
all things are put under Him, it is manifest that He is
excepted which did put all things under Him. And when all
things shall be subdued unto Him, then shall the Son also
Himself be subject unto Him that put all things under Him,
that God may be all in all." [1754]

[1747] This fragment is found in Irenæus, Hær., v. 36; but it is a mere guess that the saying of the presbyters is taken from the work of Papias.

[1748] In the future state.

[1749] The new Jerusalem on earth.

[1750] John xiv. 2.

[1751] Commentators suppose that the reference here is to Matt. xx. 23.

[1752] Matt. xxii. 10.

[1753] 1 Cor. xv. 25, 26.

[1754] 1 Cor. xv. 27, 28.

VI. [1755]

[Papias, who is now mentioned by us, affirms that he received the sayings of the apostles from those who accompanied them, and he moreover asserts that he heard in person Aristion and the presbyter John. [1756] Accordingly he mentions them frequently by name, and in his writings gives their traditions. Our notice of these circumstances may not be without its use. It may also be worth while to add to the statements of Papias already given, other passages of his in which he relates some miraculous deeds, stating that he acquired the knowledge of them from tradition. The residence of the Apostle Philip with his daughters in Hierapolis has been mentioned above. We must now point out how Papias, who lived at the same time, relates that he had received a wonderful narrative from the daughters of Philip. For he relates that a dead man was raised to life in his day. [1757] He also mentions another miracle relating to Justus, surnamed Barsabas, how he swallowed a deadly poison, and received no harm, on account of the grace of the Lord. The same person, moreover, has set down other things as coming to him from unwritten tradition, amongst these some strange parables and instructions of the Saviour, and some other things of a more fabulous nature. [1758] Amongst these he says that there will be a millennium after the resurrection from the dead, when the personal reign of Christ will be established on this earth. He moreover hands down, in his own writing, other narratives given by the previously mentioned Aristion of the Lord's sayings, and the traditions of the presbyter John. For information on these points, we can merely refer our readers to the books themselves; but now, to the extracts already made, we shall add, as being a matter of primary importance, a tradition regarding Mark who wrote the Gospel, which he [Papias] has given in the following words]: And the presbyter said this. Mark having become the interpreter of Peter, wrote down accurately whatsoever he remembered. It was not, however, in exact order that he related the sayings or deeds of Christ. For he neither heard the Lord nor accompanied Him. But afterwards, as I said, he accompanied Peter, who accommodated his instructions to the necessities [of his hearers], but with no intention of giving a regular narrative of the Lord's sayings. Wherefore Mark made no mistake in thus writing some things as he remembered them. For of one thing he took especial care, not to omit anything he had heard, and not to put anything fictitious into the statements. [This is what is related by Papias regarding

Mark; but with regard to Matthew he has made the following statements]: Matthew put together the oracles [of the Lord] in the Hebrew language, and each one interpreted them as best he could. [The same person uses proofs from the First Epistle of John, and from the Epistle of Peter in like manner. And he also gives another story of a woman [1759] who was accused of many sins before the Lord, which is to be found in the Gospel according to the Hebrews.]

 [1755] From Eusebius, Hist. Eccl., iii. 39.

[1756] [A certain presbyter, of whom see Apost. Constitutions, vii. 46, where he is said to have been ordained by St. John, the Evangelist.]

[1757] "In his day" may mean "in the days of Papias," or "in the days of Philip." As the narrative came from the daughters of Philip, it is more likely that Philip's days are meant.

[1758] [Again, note the reduplicated hearsay. Not even Irenæus, much less Eusebius, should be accepted, otherwise than as retailing vague reports.]

[1759] Rufinus supposes this story to be the same as that now found in the textus receptus of Gospel of John viii. 1-11,--the woman taken in adultery.

 VII. [1760]

Papias thus speaks, word for word: To some of them [angels] He gave dominion over the arrangement of the world, and He commissioned them to exercise their dominion well. And he says, immediately after this: but it happened that their arrangement came to nothing. [1761]

[1760] This extract is made from Andreas Cæsariensis, [Bishop of Cæsarea in Cappodocia, circiter, A.D. 500].

[1761] That is, that government of the world's affairs was a failure. An ancient writer takes taxis to mean the arraying of the evil angels in battle against God.

VIII. [1762]

With regard to the inspiration of the book (Revelation), we deem it superfluous to add another word; for the blessed Gregory Theologus and Cyril, and even men of still older date, Papias, Irenæus, Methodius, and Hippolytus, bore entirely satisfactory testimony to it.

[1762] This also is taken from Andreas Cæsariensis. [See Lardner, vol. v. 77.]

IX. [1763]

Taking occasion from Papias of Hierapolis, the illustrious, a disciple of the apostle who leaned on the bosom of Christ, and Clemens, and Pantænus the priest of [the Church] of the Alexandrians, and the wise Ammonius, the ancient and first expositors, who agreed with each other, who understood the work of the six days as referring to Christ and the whole Church.

[1763] This fragment, or rather reference, is taken from Anastasius Sinaita. Routh gives, as another fragment, the repetition of the same statement by Anastasius.

X. [1764]

(1.) Mary the mother of the Lord; (2.) Mary the wife of Cleophas or Alphæus, who was the mother of James the bishop and apostle, and of Simon and Thaddeus, and of one Joseph; (3.) Mary Salome, wife of Zebedee, mother of John the evangelist and James; (4.) Mary Magdalene. These four are found in the Gospel. James and Judas and Joseph were sons of an aunt (2) of the Lord's. James also and John were sons of another aunt (3) of the Lord's. Mary (2), mother of James the Less and Joseph, wife of Alphæus was the sister of Mary the mother of the Lord, whom John names of Cleophas, either from her father or from the family of the clan, or for some other reason. Mary Salome (3) is called Salome either from her husband or her village. Some affirm that she is the same as Mary of Cleophas, because she had two husbands.

[1764] This fragment was found by Grabe in a ms. of the Bodleian Library, with the inscription on the margin, "Papia." Westcott states that it forms part of a dictionary written by "a mediæval Papias. [He seems to have added the words, "Maria is called Illuminatrix, or Star of the Sea," etc, a middle-age device.] The dictionary exists in ms. both at Oxford and Cambridge."

Made in the USA
Las Vegas, NV
29 April 2023

71300174R00085